GOLDEN GATE
UNIVERSITY
SCHOOL OF LAW

LAW 804L – EVIDENCE LAB
Judge Lewis A. Davis
Summer 2023

Trial Evidence Skills Manual

Written by: Tim Hallahan

LAW 804L: Evidence Lab, Davis - Summer 2023
Golden Gate University

Trial Evidence Skills I:
Practical Issues

This issue I begin a multi-part series on Trial Evidence. I'll focus on the rules of evidence as an advocacy process–how to use them to win your case. A thorough understanding of the key rules that apply over and over in trial and the purpose behind those rules is crucial to success. This knowledge will help you identify what information is and is not important and credible to your factfinder, how to plead your case to ensure that the evidence with the most impact does or does not come in, how to elicit that information most powerfully, how and when to object, and how to talk the judge into the ruling you want.

The Rules. Mastering the key rules of evidence is the easy part of Trial Evidence. The Federal Rules of Evidence and the California Evidence Code are fairly simple and straightforward. Learn the key rules that arise frequently and the purpose behind those rules; don't bother memorizing technical pre-trial issues such as privilege and all of the exceptions to the secondary evidence rule–you can look those up when the time comes.

Using the Rules. The hard part of Trial Evidence is learning how to use the rules effectively and persuasively, a skill that requires preparation, especially for the inexperienced trial attorney. During step one of the preparation stage, you must clarify your goals. Are you trying to win at trial? Preserve the record for appeal? Perhaps a combination of both. Goals determine strategy, helping you decide (1) if and when to object; (2) whether or not to offer potentially objectionable evidence; (3) whether to make a motion to strike or ask for cautionary instructions; (4) how to handle *in limine* motions.

Next, anticipate the key issues. List the facts you intend to elicit, highlighting those that are questionable and making sure your authority is solid and available. Anticipate, too, the questionable evidence that opposing counsel is likely to bring out–have your authority ready on those points. Be ready to cite code sections and cases. Have a trial memo available on any key issue that may arise.

How to Object. Make clear for the judge and record (1) that you are objecting, and (2) the specific basis for the objection. In a jury trial, any discussion that's necessary will usually take place at the bench, though some judges allow fairly lengthy arguments in front of the jury, and you need to be ready to take advantage of that.

Stand up when you make your objections. Standing shows respect, gives you authority, and stops the witness in his tracks. Be affirmative, speak loud enough to be heard, and be polite to the judge.

When to Object. You should object as soon as it's clear that the question or answer is objectionable. Although many judges will permit objections a question or two late, tactically it's best to intervene before the objectionable information comes out.

Tactics. Goals dictate tactics. If your goal is to preserve the record, do the research necessary to determine whether you should object, move to strike, or request cautionary instructions as to particular evidentiary issues.

If your goal is to win at trial, you must have the answers to some key questions to help you decide whether or not to object: Will the information hurt or help? Will an objection merely highlight the importance of the information? Will it look like you're hiding something from the jury? Is there a viable alternative? How likely is it that the judge will agree?

Many attorneys object to even slightly damaging material early on. This helps establish credibility and competence with the judge, and lets opposing counsel and the witness know that you are paying attention, that they better play by the rules.

Motions in Limine. The best tool for safely eliminating objectionable material is the *in limine* motion, which should be heard on the record but before the jury is impaneled; written memoranda are desirable, and required in most jurisdictions. Motions *in limine* avoid the danger of the jury hearing inadmissible material, help preserve the record so counsel does not have to object continually before the jury, and establish counsel's credibility with the judge.

These motions may also take the form of a motion to admit, whereby counsel raises questionable material he'd like admitted but is afraid the judge will disallow if not given sufficient time to analyze the issue during the heat of trial.

Be selective in the number of issues you raise–a long list will tempt the judge to postpone her decision until the objections come up at trial. As you raise an issue, begin by telling the judge precisely what the evidence is you wish her to admit or exclude, why she should rule your way, and what you'd like her to do about it, e.g., to rule that it is inadmissible, to tell your opponent not to elicit the evidence, and to tell him to admonish his witnesses not to blurt it out.

Offers of Proof. The offer of proof is a disclosure made out of   earshot of the jury. Counsel, offering evidence to which an objection has been made, discloses (1) what the evidence is, and (2) the purpose of proving the particular facts. This allows the trial judge to evaluate the admissibility of the evidence more fully and provides a record sufficiently detailed to allow a meaningful review of the court's ruling. It's important to get to the bench with your offer of proof before the judge rules against you–people don't change their minds readily, especially in public.

Dealing with the Judge. The rules of evidence are sparse. Trial judges are given tremendous discretion by appellate courts on evidentiary issues. Good judges may rule completely differently on the exact same issues. Therefore, the premium is on the trial lawyer's ability to convince the judge of his position. If you have anticipated an issue, you'll be ready with your authority and an argument that applies the reasoning behind the applicable code section to the situation at hand.

Key is establishing your credibility with the judge early–through *in limine* motions, memoranda, and your professional attitude. In pursuit of that proper attitude, don't misstate the law, have your authority ready, don't waste time with excess verbiage and pointless objections, be efficient, and show respect to everyone in the courtroom, including the courtroom staff. Be unfailingly polite, even in the face of adverse rulings. Showing anger or disgust is disrespectful and makes counsel appear weak in the eyes of the judge and jury alike.

Next Issue.   Next time I'll turn to an issue at the core of Trial Evidence–Relevance.

Trial Evidence Skills Part II
Relevance

If you want to be an effective trial advocate, you must understand the issue of relevance. Such understanding will boost your chances of persuading a judge to admit or deny questionable evidence and will help you plead and structure your entire case.

To be relevant at trial, evidence must be probative of: (1) a witness's credibility, or (2) a material fact or issue in the trial.

Credibility. A witness's credibility is always at issue. So is that of an out-of-court hearsay declarant. Evidence that is probative of any of the witness's four testimonial capacities is generally deemed relevant. The four testimonial capacities are ability to perceive, memory, communication, and sincerity (the latter further subdivided into bias, interest, prejudice, and corruption).

In other words, each witness's testimony must be not just clear and logical, but persuasive as well. For important testimony, elicit facts that show that the witness's memory, perceptions, and conclusions are logical, complete, and accurate; and that the witness has no axe to grind. On cross-exam, show the opposite, e.g., "You were 200 yards away?" " In the two years since this happened, you've arrested over 100 other suspected drunk drivers, haven't you?" "You're the plaintiff's sister-in-law, aren't you?"

Another kind of credibility evidence that judges normally allow on direct exam is brief background information, such as the witness's age, education, residence, family, job, and outside activities. You should ask these questions if you can–jurors like witnesses more if they know more about them, and your witnesses will have a chance to warm up and get comfortable with this easy, neutral information before getting to the heart of their testimony. But don't let your witness go too far ("I worked with Mother Theresa for two years") else you invite objections, the jury's distain, or otherwise impermissible character assassination of the witness through the door she just opened.

Logical Relevance. The other type of relevant evidence is that which is *probative* of a fact or issue *material* to the case. Probative evidence tends to make the issue or fact more or less likely to have occurred or be true. Whether or not something is probative is a very low standard–"any tendency in reason" in the words of Evidence Code section 210. For example, testimony that the murderer had brown eyes is probative of who did the murder, even though it only narrows down the list of suspects to 200 million or so.

Usually the more important issue is materiality. For evidence to be material, the fact or issue to be proved must have something to do with the ultimate decision to be made, i.e., it must tie directly to a jury instruction. The above testimony about brown eyes would be material if the issue in the case was identity but not if it was a self-defense case. An attorney's gambling debts are probative of his immediate need for money, which would be material in a legal malpractice case based on misappropriating client funds but probably not on one based on his missing a statutory deadline.

Consider all the different ways that an important piece of evidence might be material. Often important information is specifically inadmissible for its most obvious purpose but may be allowed if you can articulate another basis for materiality. For example, you can't show that your opponent is insured to prove that she is liable or has deep pockets, but you can elicit evidence that her key witness is an insurance company investigator because it goes to bias. Character evidence rules say you can't show that 10 other people have slipped and fallen in the produce department at the Rockridge Safeway to prove that it is a dangerous spot, but you can offer the evidence to show notice.

Once you demonstrate materiality of any kind, the evidence becomes presumptively admissible and the burden shifts to the opponent to attempt to exclude it. The ability to come up with alternative theories of relevance is crucial to good trial lawyering–and one of the things that can make it a lot of fun.

Evidence Code Section 352. The flip side of relevance is section 352 and its federal counterpart FRE 403. Even if relevant, evidence may be excluded under the broad provisions of 352 and FRE 403, as less probative than prejudicial, confusing, time-consuming, or misleading to the jury.

Appellate courts give the trial court broad discretion in exercising these rules, so it behooves you to learn all you can about their elasticity, including, if possible, the inclinations of the trial judge. Is the judge concerned about confusing the jury? Or is wasting time her *bete noir*? Be sure to articulate why admitting the evidence is or is not a problem. "Your honor, if this evidence is admitted I'll have to put on 15 rebuttal witnesses, and we'll be here until Christmas!" The best time to raise these issues is during *in limine* motions, away from the prying ears of the jury.

Next Issue. Next time I'll turn my attention to the Form of the Question objections that occur frequently during Direct Exam.

Form of Question: Direct Examination

Form of the questions objections are mostly based on California Evidence Code section 765 and Federal Rule of Evidence 611(a). These provisions give the trial judge overall control over the trial so as to maximize speedy ascertainment of the truth and minimize witness harassment. Specific form objections that may arise during any given examination are not easy to anticipate beforehand so it's important to get a good intuitive grasp on all of them. As with most types of objections, remembering the purpose behind the rule will help you identify the problem and argue your objection effectively.

A good source for form objections with lots of examples is *California Trial Objections* (CEB 2013). Here are a few of the form objections that frequently occur during direct examination:

Leading Questions. Leading questions are those that directly suggest the desired answer to the witness. They may simply direct the witness to say "Yes", e.g., "You were enraged, weren't you?" or instead may contain such suggestive detail that the witness will merely incorporate it into his answer, e.g., "Tell us whether or not you were enraged when you saw the defendant with your wife?" The test is *not* whether or not the question can be answered "Yes" or "No."

Per EC section 767 and FRE 611(c), it is generally improper to ask leading questions on direct or redirect examination; after all, the witness is supposed to be testifying, not the lawyer. In making her ruling, the judge will weigh how leading the question is vs. how important and in dispute the evidence is.

Even if it were permissible, it's usually poor tactics to lead on direct; the witness's credibility is enhanced when the testimony comes out in his own words. Asking questions that allow the witness to answer simply "Yes" or "No" weakens the message. To avoid impermissible leading questions, and to open up the witness, begin each question with *Who, What, When, Where, How, Please describe,* or *Tell the jury…*

When are leading questions appropriate? Leading questions may be asked of a witness on cross examination or re-cross examination. You may also ask leading questions on direct for preliminary matters, refreshing recollection, and examining hostile or (in California) expert witnesses. In addition, judges typically allow lawyers to lead in these situations: transitional questions, neutral background information, foundations, and when dealing with witnesses with memory, language, or mental problems.

On the other hand, the judge may prohibit asking leading questions on cross examination when the witness is obviously biased in favor of the cross examiner and would be particularly susceptible to questions that suggest the desired answer. **Narrative.** A question that calls for a narrative response is just the opposite of the leading question. Instead of suggesting the answer to the witness, counsel is now asking a question likely to solicit a flood of information so uncontrolled that it's impossible to know when objectionable material may come out.

Narrative questions often begin with a phrase like "Tell us everything..." Counsel's attempt to let the witness tell her own story has the advantage of allowing the client to use her own words, to speak naturally, spontaneously, and believably. But it's also an invitation for the witness to launch into a rambling monologue. The overall effect may be especially negative if the story comes out in a rapid, disjointed, confusing fashion.

A proper question is more specific, sufficiently directed to inform the witness and opposing counsel precisely what type of information is being solicited. The key is to maintain control of the witness while she tells the story in her own words. Use an open-ended question with a specific focus, usually by time, e.g., "What did he do next?" or in reference to a place or object, e.g., "What did you see on the north side of the intersection?"

Even if the question doesn't call for a narrative, the witness may launch into one anyway. Don't be afraid to politely interrupt the witness with an objection if you're the opponent, or a gentle admonition if she's your witness to guide her back on track–"Excuse me, let me ask you another question here..." If you're the opponent and the answer hurts your case, you can make a motion to strike and/or ask the judge to admonish the witness to stick to the question asked.

Vague/General. Questions that are too vague or general, especially as to time, place, or person, run the risk of misleading or confusing the jury. Your #1 goal as a communicator is clarity. You must be understood by the witness and fact finder, which demands that your questions be specific. Ask simple questions, avoiding confusing pronouns. "What did they say?" is a vague question unless it is crystal clear who "they" are.

Assumes Fact not in Evidence. This common problem is difficult to recognize without practice. It is especially objectionable when the information assumed in the question is important and in dispute. The classic example: "When did you stop beating your wife?" As with the other form objections, it's better to avoid the problem by eliciting important facts clearly and distinctly. Slipping in important information by way of an impermissible question is either ineffectual, unethical or both.

Asked and Answered/Cumulative. Here the issue is efficiency. Counsel must weigh the desirability of repeating key information with its tendency to invite objection and the enmity of both judge and jury. This is one of the few objections jurors love to hear.

Next Issue. Next time I'll tackle Hearsay.

Trial Evidence Skills Part IV

Hearsay

Hearsay is the second core trial evidence issue (after Relevance) and probably the most misunderstood. The difficult issue with hearsay is not whether one of the many exceptions apply–they're straightforward and easy to get a handle on. The hard part of hearsay is identifying whether or not a statement is hearsay to begin with. The key to understanding the hearsay rule is grasping the purpose behind it–the right to cross-examination. For counsel to avoid impermissible hearsay, opposing counsel must be able to test the out-of-court statement at the time it was made against the four dangers of testimonial evidence: faulty perception, inaccurate memory, ambiguity, and insincerity. The witness or source of information must be able to be cross-examined *at the time* the information is given on these issues. Be aware of the purpose for the rule so you'll be able to make your timely objection and articulate it to your trial judge if need be. "I need to cross-examine her on how well she could see it, how well she remembered it, what she meant by 'it was his fault', and what bias or interest she might have had when she made the statement."

Three-Step Analysis. To determine whether evidence is hearsay, ask yourself these three questions: (1) Is the statement out-of-court? (2) Is it an assertion? (3) Is it being offered for the truth of the matter being asserted? In order to qualify as hearsay, all three parts of the hearsay "equation" must be met.

1. Out-of-court. A statement is out-of-court if the original source of the information is *not* the witness as she testifies at the trial. Even a previous statement by the witness herself is out-of-court. "Last week I said 'The light was green.'" An oral statement made at a prior hearing or trial is out-of-court, as are those in writings, audiotapes and videotapes made at another time.

2. Assertion. An assertion is a positive declaration, a transfer of information. "The man drove south on Broadway." "The woman bought an ice-cream cone." The mere fact that a conversation took place is not an assertion, nor is the fact that someone asserted something unless the assertion itself is elicited. "The paramedic advised me of her condition" is not a problem, what the paramedic actually said is. Questions are usually not assertions, nor are directives, e.g., "I told him to go to the store." However, they may contain an implied assertion and become a problem, e.g., "I asked him why he was driving so fast."

Nonverbal conduct can be an assertion only if it is intended to be so, as in this example: "The victim pointed at the defendant when I asked her if she saw the man who did it." On the other hand, "The paralegal looked down at the unconscious victim and shook his head" would not be an assertion because none was intended. Make one little change, however–"The paralegal looked up at me and shook his head"–and it becomes an intentional assertion.

Sometimes even silence can be an assertion. "I asked the crowd if anyone saw anything, and nobody answered."

3. Truth of the Matter Asserted. This concept is the key to hearsay. Not all out-of-court statements are hearsay, and probably not even most, because a good trial lawyer can usually find another reason to offer the evidence besides *for the truth of the matter asserted.*

For example, "The passenger said the light was red" is hearsay only when offered to show that the light was red.   It is not hearsay if it is probative of another material fact–for example, the passenger could see or speak, was not color-blind, was a liar, the light was operating, the witness could hear, or the driver should have stopped when she heard that the light was red.

There are four main reasons why out-of-court assertions are not offered for the truth:

Operative words.   An out-of-court statement may be permissible hearsay if the words themselves have legal significance just by being said.   For example: "I accept your offer," or "Go ahead, search the car," or "You have the right to remain silent. Everything you say may be used against you..."

The effect on the hearer.   Take, for example, a murder case, where the defendant, pleading self-defense, testifies that he had been told the victim had a loaded gun, had threatened him, and had previously killed five people.   Those assertions are not being offered for their truth, but rather to show that the defendant was scared and took reasonable action given what he'd heard.

Circumstantial evidence of the declarant's thoughts or actions.   The classic example is the declarant saying "I am Napoleon."   It's being offered to show that the declarant is crazy, not that he's Napoleon.   Another example: the defendant's girlfriend testifies that the defendant told her that "Ortiz is a narc."   This is not offered for the truth of the matter asserted–that Ortiz was a narc–but rather to show that the defendant *thought* Ortiz was a narc and therefore never would have sold drugs to him.

Completion.   In many situations you can offer a statement to show completion.   Evidence Code section 356 and FRE 106 allow out-of-court assertions to show why the parties acted a certain why or to provide the other side of the conversation.

Just because your opponent has very cleverly articulated one of these four bases for why the out-of-court assertion is not offered for its truth, don't give up on your hearsay objection.   If it will be difficult for the jury to take the evidence purely for its non-hearsay purpose, argue that the court should exclude it all together per Evidence Code section 352 or FRE 403.   Cite the Law Revision Commission Notes to section 355 as your authority.

Next Month.   Next issue I'll discuss the most important Hearsay Exceptions.

TRIAL EVIDENCE -- PART V

Hearsay Exceptions

Hearsay exceptions are based on a combination of reliability and need. The justification for most exceptions is that cross-examination is unnecessary to test one or more of the out-of-court declarant's four testimonial capacities– perception, memory, communication, sincerity. For example, *statements of presently felt mental or physical state* (EC 1250) are admissible because perception is an element of the foundation and their spontaneous nature makes it unnecessary to cross-examine regarding memory and sincerity. Where there is less inherent reliability, e.g., *declarations against interest* (EC 1230), the proponent must demonstrate more need for the evidence at trial, usually in the form of the declarant's unavailability. Be able to articulate why an exception should or should not apply by addressing the need to cross-examine and how vital the evidence is.

The principal exceptions:

1. Admissions. The party admission exception (EC 1220) should really be titled "statements of a party." Any statement of a party, if relevant, may be offered against that party; it need not be an "admission" in the classical meaning of the word. Note that you can offer only another party's statements, not your own.

Admissions can be authorized–that is, made by someone else on the party's behalf, if that person is authorized to make that or similar statements concerning the subject matter.

An admission can be implied by a response to someone else's statement. For example: "I told the defendant that I knew he robbed that bank, and he replied that the gun wasn't loaded." EC 1221. Similarly, admissions can be adopted by silence if the statement is made under circumstances in which one would ordinarily deny it if it weren't true. "He said nothing when I accused him of robbing the bank." However, it is important that the party was in a position to see and hear the accusation, that she was not intimidated, and that she had not been warned that what she said could be used against her.

The admissions exception can often be used to bootstrap in evidence normally inadmissible for other reasons, such as opinions and information of which the party has no personal knowledge.

2. Prior Statements. Pretrial statements of witnesses usually fall within the hearsay rule and are inadmissible. However, when the witness has made a prior statement that is inconsistent with his or her testimony at trial or hearing, the *prior inconsistent statement* is not made inadmissible by the hearsay rule. EC 1235. Usually prior inconsistent statements are offered during cross-examination of that witness. When offered extrinsically, the proponent must comply with EC 770 which mandates that the witness had been given an opportunity, while being examined, to explain or deny the prior inconsistent statement or that he not have been excused yet. Accordingly, when a judge asks whether an opponent's witness may be excused, reply that due to EC 770 you ask that she be available on a telephone-standby basis.

3. Declarations Against Interest. This exception applies to nonparties whose statements are so contrary to their pecuniary, penal or social interest that they are unlikely to have been made if untrue. As noted above, be prepared to establish unavailability. EC 1230.

4. Spontaneous Statements. These fit within what many of us think of as the "excited utterance" exception. To qualify, the statement must describe an event or condition perceived by the declarant while he's still under the excitement caused by experiencing it. EC 1240.

5. Contemporaneous Statements. These are statements made by the declarant offered to explain what he's doing while he's doing it. EC 1241. Lawyers and judges often confuse this exception, the *spontaneous statement*, and the *statement of mental or physical state*, lumping them together in the commonly heard refrain "it goes to state of mind." When this happens, your response in turn should be "who's state of mind and how is it relevant?"

Other issues:

1. Multiple Hearsay. When a statement consists of several layers of assertions– "The bystander told me that the victim said the light was green"–it may be admitted provided each out-of-court statement is non-hearsay or meets the requirements of an exception to the hearsay rule. If one fails, they all fail. Business and official records often contain multiple layers of hearsay, all of which must be analyzed.

2. Unavailability. Several hearsay exceptions require, as a condition for admissibility, that the declarant be unavailable as a witness. EC 240. Note that unavailability can apply to a witness who is present or even testifying if, say, her memory has failed or she is exerting a privilege. Judges have loads of discretion in determining unavailability. Be sure to create a paper trail, tracking how much effort you've put into trying to get the witness to court.

Next Issue

Next time I'll discuss Exhibits.

TRIAL EVIDENCE   Part 6

Exhibits

Exhibits are crucial in most trials: they seem to have more inherent credibility than oral testimony, they go into the jury room or judge's chambers when the verdict is being decided, most people learn and retain 5 times better from their eyes than ears, and exhibits enhance the general visual appeal and impact of your case. Accordingly, a good trial lawyer should know how to offer and object to exhibits as both an evidence technician and an advocate.

Planning

Select carefully which exhibits you will use and scrutinize them for extraneous information which might be otherwise inadmissible or detract from the essence of your case. Scrutinize your opponent's proposed exhibits as well. Plan to weave the introduction of your exhibits into the context of the case so the jury will understand their importance. For example, have the witness describe how she got to the accident scene before the photo is introduced. Figure out ahead of time how you will display your exhibits to the jury so that everyone can see them.

Mechanical Steps

The key to introducing exhibits is learning how to do it smoothly and quickly, thereby avoiding needless objections and impressing judge, jury, and opposing counsel with your competence. Hon. Ken Kawaichi calls your preliminary steps the *Magic Triangle*: show the proposed exhibit to your opponent, ask to have the exhibit marked "for identification", ask to approach the witness, ask the witness to identify the item as you hand it to him, return to your table and lay the foundation. Check with your judge pretrial to see how she likes all of these steps done; some may be unnecessary, if, for example, she wants all exhibits pre-marked.

The Foundation

You don't have to memorize the foundation for every type of exhibit. Sources like *California Evidentiary Foundations* by Prof. Edward Imwinkelried (Matthew Bender) or CEB's *Effective Introduction of Evidence in California* will provide the script you need. Refer to one right before trial and practice with each exhibit. Bring the source to court as a backup.

Crucial to laying a foundation for an exhibit, or objecting to it, is to understand why a foundation is necessary. If you understand the evidentiary issues, you can get out of trouble if you or a witness can't mouth the exact words the judge is looking for.

Use the tests of *relevance, authenticity, hearsay,* and *best evidence* to analyze each potential exhibit.

- *Relevance*: Is it probative of a material issue in the case or to the credibility of a witness?

- *Authentication*: What is it? How does the witness know what it is? Is it in the same relevant condition? If it isn't the exact same thing, is it a true and accurate reflection of it?

- *Hearsay*: If there are words on it, are those words offered for the truth of the matter they assert? If so, does an exception apply?

- *Best Evidence*: Is it being offered to prove the contents of a "writing" as defined by the code? If so, is it the "original" as defined? If not, does one of many exceptions arise? Best Evidence is rarely a trial issue, but when it is, it can be outcome-determinative.

The most important foundations to know well are for business and official records, refreshed and recorded recollection, and prior inconsistent statements.

Offering and Showing

After you've laid the foundation, offer the exhibit. Then ask to show it. Make sure you've arranged for it to be seen by everyone by making individual copies, or a blowup, or by using an overhead projector or some sort of presentation software. If the judge will not rule on admissibility until the end of your examination or case, ask that the jury be allowed to see it now while the exhibit makes most sense in the context of your examination. Also, make sure you offer it later and get your ruling.

Final Argument

Use your exhibits during final argument. They have loads of credibility, they provide visual impact, and they give you nice props. Tell the jurors to look at the exhibits during deliberation. And be sure, after all of your hard work, that they actually make it into the jury room.

Trial Evidence Part 7
by Tim Hallahan

Competence and Opinion

Competence

Competence relates to witnesses, not to evidence. Two issues arise: (1) Is the witness competent to testify about a particular subject? (2) Is she competent to testify at all?

Competence as to Subject Matter

The offering party must provide sufficient evidence of a witness's personal knowledge of the facts about which she will testify before she does so. EC 702. The burden is to provide enough evidence so that the judge can determine that a jury could reasonably find personal knowledge. EC 403.

The proponent must establish the first two of each witness's four testimonial capacities–that the witness perceived the fact (*perception*) and can testify about it from his own present recollection (*memory*). Such knowledge can be established from the witness's own testimony or from any other admissible evidence; but merely asking the witness if he has personal knowledge is insufficient.

However, you'd never get through a trial if you established this foundation for every fact. You need to provide it only if there is an objection. Although judges rarely sustain objections as to personal knowledge if even a minimal showing is made, you should try to be as convincing as possible. If the evidence is important, provide a solid foundation for the witness's ability to (1) observe details of the event, and (2) remember them accurately. "I was ten feet away. It stands out in my memory because I've never seen anything like that before or since."

It's necessary to establish personal knowledge for all witnesses except for qualified experts, who may base their opinions on facts about which they have no such knowledge.

Competence as a Witness

Every person is qualified to be a witness, irrespective of age, and no person is disqualified to testify to any matter, except as provided by statute (e.g., judges). Here the burden is on the opponent to establish that the witness does not have the third or fourth testimonial capacity–that she is incapable of communicating information understandably (*communication*) or does not understand her duty to tell the truth (*sincerity*). Children or people suffering from mental disabilities are *not* presumed to be incompetent.

If the opponent objects on this basis, the court will hold a hearing. Only a clear showing of incompetency will disqualify the witness. So if you intend to object, you'll probably need an expert.

Lay Opinion

Generally a lay witness may testify only to facts she has personally observed; the factfinder's job is to draw inferences and conclusions from those facts. Occasionally, however, the line between fact and opinion blurs. And sometimes the factfinder, in order to do the job well, needs to hear opinions from the witness. Therefore, the rules as to lay opinion testimony have been relaxed over the years. As a general rule, judges allow lay opinions if they are based on the witness's own personal observations and are the type of conclusions lay people reliably draw in their everyday life, e.g., "The car was going over 70 miles per hour," "He looked drunk." EC 800

Permissible lay opinions can be sorted into those involving (1) **Collective Fact**, and (2) **Skilled Observer**. Collective fact opinions are conclusions that cannot be broken down into more incremental facts that can be easily verbalized or understood. The requirements are that (1) the witness personally observed the underlying factual data and drew from it a rational conclusion of the type that he and other lay people normally draw, and (2) the conclusion will be more helpful to the jury than merely the underlying data. Common examples include height, weight, identity, and distance.

The admissibility of the opinions of a skilled observer must meet the same requirements as above; in addition, judges often require more foundation in terms of experience than can be assumed from everyday living. For example, identifying a signature demands a showing of familiarity and experience with the person's handwriting.

With both types of opinion, judges tend to err on the side of admissibility, leaving it to opposing counsel to demonstrate the unreliability of the conclusions on cross-examination. However, the closer the evidence comes to the ultimate issue in the case, the stricter the standard the judge will apply. The same principle applies to trial advocacy: the more important the evidence, the more concrete and fact-based the testimony should be.

Next Time

Next issue, I'll discuss Form of the Question objections.

HOT BONUS

Try your hand at *I Object!* and *I Object Again!: Criminal*, my two online Qstream evidence course. Go to www.QStream.com, sign up, and, over the course of a month or so, two questions will appear in your email box every few days. You can practice making rulings and sharpen your evidence knowledge. It's fun, educational, and free.

Tim Hallahan is Director of the Trial Advocacy Program at Stanford Law School, a judicial education attorney with the California Judicial Council, a national CLE speaker, and cofounder of The Hecht Training Group, a litigation skills training firm (http://www.hechttraininggroup.com). He also serves on the ACBA CAAP Training Committee.

Trial Evidence 8

Form of the Question: Cross-Exam

Two types of questions are generally permissible on cross-examination: (1) questions that impeach the witness's credibility, and (2) questions designed to elicit other relevant facts relative to the general scope of the direct examination. Because cross-examination is such an important part of our trial system and because of its inherent difficulty, judges tend to give attorneys wide latitude regarding the form of the questions they may ask on cross-examination.

EC 765 and FRE 611(a) give judges the authority to control the examination of witnesses, an authority they are likely to exercise only when questions are misleading, unfair, or unnecessarily time-consuming or harassing.

As with most areas of trial evidence, these rules dictate how the lawyer *should* ask her questions   from an advocacy as well as evidentiary standpoint.   Improper questioning leads to loss of control, interruption with objections, and antagonism from the judge and jury.   The best questioning on cross-examination is simple and direct, both in words and sentence structure.

Consider these main problem areas:

Harassment.   Although most cross-examination necessarily involves some harassment, EC 765 authorizes judges to protect witnesses from "undue harassment or embarrassment."   Judges, who have a duty to step in and interrupt even if counsel doesn't object, usually base their rulings on whether the issue concerns important facts in the case, how early it comes in the cross-exam, and how much the witness needs protection.

Vague/General.   The real danger with vague or overly broad questions is that they allow counsel to argue to the jury things that the witness never intended by her answers.   In fact, many attorneys coach their witnesses to take advantage of broad or vague questions by forcefully arguing their version of the facts.

Ambiguous.   This type of question is objectionable for the same reason as vague questions—the witness's words may be offered for a meaning she never intended.   On cross-exam the lawyer is really doing the testifying with leading questions, so ambiguous questions add up to bad advocacy.

Argumentative.   Proper examination is designed to elicit relevant information. A question is improperly argumentative if counsel is (1) arguing with the witness; (2) eliciting an argument in response to his question; or (3) asking the witness to accept his inference or interpretation of proven or assumed facts.   Questions can be argumentative in tone as well as phrasing.   Argumentative questions often begin with phrases such as "Are you asking us to believe...?"   "Are you trying to tell us...?"   Reserve argument for closing argument.

Asked and Answered.   Attorneys during direct examination are generally allowed to elicit a piece of information from a witness only once.   This keeps the trial moving and precludes undue focus on one issue.   The cross-examiner, however, is often given more latitude, especially if multiple questions will help the factfinder determine the truth.   Be careful though—the only objections jurors say they like to hear are "asked and answered", "cumulative", and "repetitive."

Misstating Previous Testimony.   It is both objectionable and unethical to misquote a witness's previous testimony.   Make it clear to the factfinder if your opponent engages in such behavior.

Compound Questions.   Counsel should ask only one question at a time. Again, the danger is that the witness or factfinder will be misled.   A "yes" answer may apply only to the first part of the question and not to the second. The danger to the *questioner* is that the factfinder may not understand the whole question or may miss its significance, which probably wouldn't happen if several separate questions were asked.

Non-responsive Answers.   In most states, either party can move to strike an answer that does not directly respond to the question.   Judges usually grant the motion unless: (1) the volunteered information is clearly relevant; (2) otherwise admissible; and (3) will inevitably be elicited later from this witness.   Many federal judges will grant such a motion only if it is the examining attorney who moves to strike.   Cross-examiners should not lose sight of the importance of this motion as a means of controlling witnesses.   If necessary, firmly but politely interrupt the non-responsive answer and move to strike.

Tactics of Objecting
Many experienced trial attorneys rarely object on cross-examination, because: (1) judges tend to give attorneys wide latitude on cross; (2) they don't want to appear to be protecting their witness; (3) a well-prepared witness may turn an improperly phrased question to her advantage and launch into an unwanted narrative; and (4) the jury can usually recognize when questions are unfair or counsel is being abusive.

Reserve your objections for those times when the danger of misleading the witness or factfinder is real or when your witness needs a break.

Next Time
Next issue, I'll discuss Impeachment.

Tim Hallahan is Director of the Trial Advocacy Program at Stanford Law School, a Judicial Education Attorney with the California Judicial Council, a national CLE speaker, and cofounder of The Hecht Training Group, a litigation skills training firm (http://www.hechttraininggroup.com). He also serves on the ACBA CAAP Training Committee.

Trial Evidence 9

Impeachment

When you cross-examine a witness, you're generally trying to (1) elicit relevant information, or (2) impeach the witness's credibility.   Key to impeaching a witness is control.   It's usually best, therefore, to ask only those questions to which you can correctly anticipate the answers.

You may attack the witness's credibility either as a witness in general or in regard to facts she has testified to on direct exam.   The witness may be impeached directly on cross-examination, or indirectly through other witnesses or evidence.

The most important types of impeachment evidence involve (1) the four testimonial capacities; (2) prior inconsistent statements; (3) specific contradiction of the witness's testimony on direct exam; and (4) character evidence (to be covered next month).   Evidence Code section 780 and the civil and criminal jury instructions (CACI 107, CALCRIM 105) tell you what to look for.

Four Testimonial Capacities.   Proper impeachment begins with the four testimonial capacities: (1) ability or opportunity to perceive ("You weren't wearing your glasses that day, were you?"); (2)   ability to remember ("This happened two years ago?   You've investigated 400 traffic accidents since that date, haven't you?"); (3) ability to communicate clearly ("When you say you 'don't recall', do you mean that it didn't happen or that it may have happened but you don't now recall?"); and (4) sincerity.

We can challenge a witness's sincerity in four ways: (1) bias (witness favors one party); (2) prejudice (witness dislikes one party); (3) interest (financial or otherwise in outcome); and (4) corruption (witness compensated for testimony).

Prior Inconsistent Statements.   If used properly, prior inconsistent statements can be a powerful tool for impeachment and witness control.   Evidence of prior inconsistent statements may be offered (1) directly through the witness herself; (2) through another witness's testimony; or (3) through introduction of the contents of a writing, transcript or tape recording.   Even the attorney calling the witness may impeach with a prior statement.   A nontestifying hearsay declarant can be also be impeached with a prior inconsistent statement.

There are important limits on the use of prior inconsistent statements.   It must be shown that the prior statement is inconsistent with the witness's express or implied testimony at the hearing.   The judge has broad discretion to define "implied" inconsistency.   Try to make the impeachment as precise as possible for both strategic and evidentiary reasons.   If the witness now says she doesn't remember, with no other signs of evasiveness or fabrication, the prior statement cannot be admitted as a prior inconsistent statement.

When impeaching the witness through her own testimony, you need not reveal the prior statement to the witness before confronting her with it, but you must, upon request, show or disclose it to opposing counsel.   On the other hand, before counsel offers extrinsic evidence of a prior inconsistent statement, the witness must be given an opportunity to explain or deny the statement or have not yet been excused.   EC 770.

A good method of impeaching is use of the "Three C's":
>**Confirm** the testimony you'd like to impeach. "On direct exam you said ...?"
>**Credit** the prior statement to make it look like it is more likely to be accurate.   "You came into my office for a deposition?   You were under oath?   Your attorney ..."
>**Confront** with the inconsistency.   "Your Honor, reading from page 23 lines 18-22 of the witness's deposition testimony ..."

Though you may impeach with minor inconsistencies, experienced attorneys usually reserve it for more important facts.   Impeaching with minutia looks weak and impolite.   Go after the little inconsistencies only at the beginning of the cross-exam to establish control or if there are so many inconsistencies that the witness will lose all credibility.

Specific impeachment
EC 780(i) allows the cross-examiner to prove that any fact testified to by the witness is untrue, regardless of whether it's relevant to the case or otherwise inadmissible.   If the witness raises it on direct exam, it becomes fair game; however, counsel is not allowed to elicit a collateral fact from the witness on cross merely for the purpose of contradicting that testimony with other evidence. So advise your witnesses well regarding what they volunteer on direct ("I've never been in trouble before") and listen to opposing witnesses carefully so you can jump on their mistakes ("On direct you said you'd never been in trouble before?   Well, how about ...")

Final argument
Many cases are swearing contests–between witnesses and between lawyers.   If you use CACI 107 or CALCRIM 105 when you explain your impeachment to the judge and jury, applying the facts you've elicited to elements of these witness credibility instructions, you and your arguments may well end up with the most credibility of all.

Next Time
Next issue, I'll discuss Character Evidence.

Tim Hallahan is Director of the Trial Advocacy Program at Stanford Law School, a Judicial Education Attorney with the California Judicial Council, a national CLE speaker, and cofounder of The Hecht Training Group, a litigation skills training firm (http://www.hechttraininggroup.com). He also serves on the ACBA CAAP Training Committee.

Trial Evidence 10

Character Evidence in Civil Trials

Character evidence is evidence that suggests that a person or entity has a propensity to act in a certain way. It's powerful evidence, so powerful that it tends to overwhelm everything else. In addition, opening up the issue of someone or something's character can be very time-consuming. And the legal issues are complicated. Accordingly, judges in civil cases are very reluctant to allow character evidence, even when there's authority for its admission.

But good lawyers don't let this reluctance get in the way. They know that character evidence, by the very fact of its persuasive power, provides a tremendous opportunity, so they do their research, scour their cases for any chance to inject it, and present well-reasoned authority to the trial judge with plenty of advance notice so she can be comfortable ruling in their favor.

Methods of Proof. When character is admissible, there are three main ways to prove it: (1) prior or subsequent acts; (2) reputation; and (3) opinion. EC 1100, FRE 405. *Acts* are proved by a witness with personal knowledge or by a document such as a record of criminal conviction. A *reputation* character witness usually must show he has been in the same residential, social or business community as the subject, that the subject has a reputation for the particular trait within that community, and that the witness knows of the reputation. EC 1324, FRE 803(21). An *opinion* character witness must show that he knows the subject well enough to have formed a reliable opinion of the relevant character trait, and that he actually has an opinion.

Purpose. The first question to ask in analyzing the admissibility of character evidence is why it's being offered. Character evidence is usually offered for one of three purposes: (1) as a material issue in the case; (2) to show someone's behavior was consistent with the trait on a specific date; (3) as relevant to someone's credibility as a witness.

Material Issue. Character evidence is admissible when character is a material issue in the case. In a slander or libel case, for example, reputation and damage to reputation are at the heart of the matter, as is the truth of the accusation. Negligent entrustment is another type of case where character is a material issue. For example, the school district should have known better than to hire the town drunk to drive the school bus. When admissible on this basis, character generally may be proved by acts, reputation and opinion.

Conduct on a Specific Occasion. In civil cases, character evidence offered to show that someone must have acted in conformity with that propensity on a specific occasion ("if he did it before, he did it again this time") is inadmissible. EC 1101(a) The only exception is for habits. EC 1105 and FRE 406 allow propensity evidence if the activity is so frequent and regular that it can be considered a habit or custom. The activity must be specific and consistent, almost automatic. When admitted for this purpose, the evidence is proved by someone with knowledge ("I always buckle my seatbelt," "We always record the checks in the ledger").

Credibility. Evidence relating to a witness's honesty, truthfulness or veracity may be admitted regarding the witness's credibility. No other character traits are admissible for credibility. Either side may attack or support a witness's character regarding credibility; however, the witness's character may not be supported until *after* it has been attacked. EC 785, 786, 790, 1101(c), FRE 607, 608.

When a character witness testifies that another witness has a good character for truth and veracity through either reputation or opinion, that witness's testimony may be impeached with questions about whether she "has heard" of *specific* instances of the witness-at-issue's bad character. "Have you heard that Mr. Babble lied on his civil-service exam last October?"

Generally, a witness's truthfulness cannot be attacked or supported by specific acts of that witness. A limited exception in federal court [FRE 608(b)] allows cross-examination if the questioned instances are probative of truthfulness. But if the witness denies the prior bad behavior, the cross-examiner cannot prove otherwise extrinsically.

Under EC 788 and FRE 609, a greater exception exists for certain criminal convictions. Judges tend to interpret this rule narrowly in civil cases. The following factors are important: (1) how recent the conviction is; (2) how much it reflects dishonesty (embezzlement vs drug possession); (3) how likely is it to mislead or confuse the jury (its similarity to the conduct at issue); and in criminal cases, (4) how likely is it that its admission will keep the defendant from testifying.

You may prove the conviction only by cross-examining the witness or by introducing the record of judgment. In California, evidence is limited to name of felony, date and place of conviction. You must have the record in hand before asking about it, or must have a good-faith basis for believing that it occurred. You cannot use such convictions if they are constitutionally defective or if the witness has been relieved of the consequences through a pardon or other procedural devices.

"Non-character" purposes. EC 1101(b) and FRE 404(b) provide a fourth general category of purposes for which character evidence is frequently offered. This type of evidence is particularly powerful and provides a great opportunity and danger for civil and criminal lawyers. I'll discuss it in detail next issue.

Tim Hallahan is Director of the Trial Advocacy Program at Stanford Law School, a Judicial Education Attorney with the California Judicial Council, a national CLE speaker, and cofounder of The Hecht Training Group, a litigation skills training firm (http://www.hechttraininggroup.com). He also serves on the ACBA CAAP Training Committee.

Trial Evidence Part 11

Using Character Evidence for "Non-character" Purposes

California Evidence Code section 1101(b) and it's federal counterpart, FRE 404(b), allow the attorney to offer similar behavior of a person or entity if "relevant to prove some fact (such as motive, opportunity....) other than his or her disposition to commit such an act." In doing so, these rules provide both significant opportunity and danger. Character evidence is overwhelmingly persuasive, and these provisions supply the trial lawyer with the means and authority to introduce evidence containing otherwise impermissible propensity inferences.

There are number of important issues here to keep in mind. First, these evidence provisions apply to civil as well as criminal cases. The similar acts need not be crimes. EC 1101(b) says the past behavior may consist of "a crime, civil wrong, or other act." A review of the section on 1101(b) in Witkins California Evidence (5th ed, Thomson Reuters) will provide many many examples of civil cases in which EC 1101(b) acts were allowed.

Second, by prefacing the list of permissible purposes for which other acts may be offered with "such as", the statutes indicate that their lists aren't exclusive. Analyze your case carefully to find relevant non-character purposes for which prior or subsequent behavior of your opponent may be offered. For example, the fact that five people have fallen in the same spot in the local Safeway can't come in to show that it's a dangerous place, but it can come in to show knowledge–a permitted EC 1101(b) purpose. Obviously, the jury will draw both the permissible and impermissible inferences. Go to an exhaustive source of case law such as Witkins and look for cases and fact patterns similar to yours for ideas.

Perhaps you may decide to plead your case a certain way in ensure that similar acts come in. For example, prior acts of her negligence might not come in if you sue only the doctor for malpractice, but would come in if you sue the hospital for negligently entrusting that doctor with its operating facilities. In a products liability case, you might ask for punitive damages so you can put on evidence of other complaints and law suits to show notice of the defect. On the other hand, be careful that your pleadings don't open the door to otherwise impermissible prior bad conduct by *your* client.

People v. Ewoldt, 7 Cal. 4th 380 (1994) is particularly instructive. It provides a detailed analysis of EC 1101(b), the three main categories of similar acts it allows (those going to intent, identity, and plan), and the necessary degree of frequency and similarity of the other behavior compared to the that alleged in the instant case. As a general rule, other acts going to a mental state (e.g., intent, knowledge, or mistake) need a lower level of similarity and frequency, those going to plan or pattern a mid-level, and those going to identity a high degree of frequency and similarity.

Civil trial judges are reluctant to admit character evidence of any kind and not used to lawyers offering EC 1101(b) evidence. Accordingly, it's a good idea to give your trial judge as much notice as possible. Brief the issue carefully. Consider bringing a motion to admit during *in limine* motions. Be prepared to deflect your opponent's argument that the jury will be prejudiced or misled, drawing the impermissible rather than permissible inference. And let the judge know that it won't take much time to prove the similar behavior.

Criminal lawyers know how devastating EC 1101(b) and FRE 404(b) evidence can be. Some who have switched to the civil arena say that this is the most neglected area of opportunity in the evidence rules for the civil trial bar. Use it to your advantage.

Tim Hallahan is Director of the Trial Advocacy Program at Stanford Law School, a Judicial Education Attorney with the California Judicial Council, a national CLE speaker, and cofounder of The Hecht Training Group, a litigation skills training firm (http://www.hechttraininggroup.com). He also serves on the ACBA CAAP Training Committee.

Trial Evidence 12

Evidence Excluded for Policy Reasons

The California Evidence Code, Federal Rules of Evidence and case law provide that certain evidentiary areas, though relevant, may be excluded at trial because their relevance is outweighed by policy considerations. Be at least generally aware of the types of evidence excluded for policy reasons, then study them more carefully when preparing for trial.

Very importantly, keep in mind that these provisions exclude evidence only when it's offered for a particular purpose–evidence that is inadmissible when offered for one purpose may be admissible for another. As with much of evidence, this is an area where your creativity may be crucial. For example:

Subsequent Remedial Conduct. After an event, if remedial measures are taken by a party, which, if taken previously, would have made the event less likely to occur, evidence of the subsequent measures is not admissible to prove negligence or culpable conduct in connection with the event. Cal. EC 1151, FRE 407. The purpose of this exclusion is to avoid discouraging parties from taking steps to avoid future injuries. (Note that this rule does not apply to repairs undertaken by a nonparty in the action.)

On the other hand, such remedial conduct may very well be admissible if offered for another purpose–say, to impeach, to show ownership or control, or to show the feasibility of precautionary measures, if controverted. For example, evidence that a store owner subsequently repaired the steps in question might be admissible to show that he owned the place or to impeach his credibility if he testifies that the steps were safe or that he did everything possible to prevent an accident.

Offers to Compromise. Evidence of conduct or statements made in compromise negotiations is usually not admissible to prove liability or the invalidity of a claim. This policy exclusion seeks to encourage parties to settle their disputes. Cal. EC 1152, FRE 408, 409.

Excluded, for example, would be evidence of (1) furnishing–or offering or promising to furnish, or (2) accepting–or offering or promising to accept, a valuable consideration while attempting to compromise a claim. Note that offers to compromise and statements made in negotiation apply to nonparties as well as to parties.

Cal EC 1153 and FRE 410 make a criminal defendant's offer to plead guilty, or an actual guilty plea that is later withdrawn, inadmissible in any proceeding.

Of course, this rule does not require the exclusion of any evidence otherwise discoverable merely because it came up in a compromise negotiation. Nor does it require exclusion when the evidence is offered for a purpose other than proving or disproving the validity of the disputed claim–say, showing bias or prejudice, or countering a contention of undue delay.

The exclusion also does not apply to statements made before the negotiation started or after it ended, though that can be difficult to determine.   If you're concerned about making what might be construed as an admission while discussing your case with your opponent, make it clear that you are speaking hypothetically, especially if you are dealing with someone with questionable ethics or someone you don't know.   To be especially safe, put your disclaimer in writing.

Insurance.   Evidence of insurance coverage is not admissible to prove negligence or other wrongdoing.   This policy aims (1) to avoid discouraging parties from obtaining insurance, and (2) to avoid jurors awarding damages based on an ability to pay.   Cal EC 1155, FRE 411.

Insurance coverage may be admissible for purposes other than proving negligence.   It's admissible if it's an integral part of another piece of evidence of substantial importance, as in this defendant's statement to a plaintiff: "I have insurance so don't bother to get names and addresses of witnesses."   It is also permissible to show the bias of an insurance investigator testifying for the insured party.

Dealing with the trial judge.   Judges have broad discretion when applying these rules.   Most are very reluctant to admit this type of evidence even when you are offering it other than for the prohibited purpose.   If you want to get it in, give the judge plenty of warning, and give her your case authority in writing.   On the flip side, if you want to keep it out, argue that the jury cannot realistically take it only for its permitted purpose.   Urge the judge to follow the advice of the Law Revision Commission Comment to Cal. EC section 355 which suggests that judges use their discretion to exclude evidence when they think jurors cannot accept it for the limited purpose offered.

Tim Hallahan is Director of the Trial Advocacy Program at Stanford Law School, a Judicial Education Attorney with the California Judicial Council, a national CLE speaker, and cofounder of The Hecht Training Group, a litigation skills training firm (http://www.hechttraininggroup.com). He also serves on the ACBA CAAP Training Committee.

Motions in Limine:
Not Just Billable Events

Some lawyers think *"in limine"* refers exclusively to motions to "limit" prospective trial evidence. Others think it means "last great pretrial billable event." Actually, *"in limine"* is Latin for "on the threshold." These last pretrial motions can do much more than limit evidence, and therefore you should look at them as your first great trial advocacy event.

Most motions *in limine* do aim to eliminate objectionable material. By bringing such a motion you seek to 1) avoid the danger of the jury hearing inadmissible material, and 2) preserve the record so you don't have to object continually before the jury. Be sure to raise issues concerning evidence that would be especially powerful and thus impossible for the jury to ignore, even when instructed to do so—e.g. EC §352, hearsay, and character evidence. Judges especially welcome motions that might preclude entire areas of testimony—for example, on the basis of relevance or lack of witness expertise. Raise these even in court trials. Judges do not welcome motions based on vague grounds or motions that do not specify the exact testimony or evidence anticipated. "I object to anything counsel intends to offer that is speculative or lacks foundation." If the motion will require an EC §402 hearing, be sure that you've lined up your witnesses.

Motions *in limine* may also seek to admit evidence—sometimes called "motions to admit." With this type of motion counsel raises questionable material he'd like admitted but is afraid the judge will disallow if not given sufficient time to analyze the issue before the heat of trial. The danger of raising it before trial is, of course, that opposing counsel will be warned and ready to respond. However, if the situation is novel or complicated and you have good authority, raise it yourself first. For example, lawyers and judges generally assume that character evidence is inadmissible in civil cases. However, a glance at Witkin's California Evidence reveals many instances where EC §1101(b) prior-acts evidence has been ruled admissible in civil trials. If you offer the evidence for the first time during trial, you risk an adverse ruling. Raise it *in limine* with written authority, and the judge is more likely to get it right. Plus, she'll appreciate your giving her the time to think about it.

Be selective in the number of issues you raise. A long list will tempt the judge to postpone his decision until the objections come up at trial. As you raise an issue, begin by telling the judge precisely what evidence you wish him to admit or exclude, why he should rule your way, and what you'd like him to do about it—namely to rule that it is inadmissible, tell your opponent not to elicit the evidence, and to admonish her witnesses not to blurt it out.

If your motion to exclude is denied, ask for a stipulation that you have made your record so that you need not raise an objection at trial in order to preserve it. If you do not receive such a stipulation, the safest bet is to object again when applicable during the trial. See EC §353 and *People v. Morris* (1991) 53 Cal.3d 152, 189-190 for more specifics. If your motion to admit is denied, be sure to make an offer of proof outlining exactly what that evidence would be, again so you can make your record for appeal.

Be sure to raise your *in limine* motions before jury selection. You want to know what evidence will be allowed before you begin jury *voir dire* and opening statements so you will know what you and your opponent should and should not discuss. Written memoranda are desirable, and required in most jurisdictions. Make sure your motion is on the record. If you have a judge who insists on holding informal discussions in chambers, be sure to have the discussions summarized for the record later.

The final good reason for concentrating on your motions *in limine* is that they provide a great means of seizing and maintaining momentum. Remember, a trial is like a ball game—grab momentum early, and you're likely to keep it to the end. Doing a forceful and compelling job raising and arguing these initial issues will establish your credibility with both judge and opponent. Don't waste the opportunity.

CHAPTER 10

THE HEARSAY RULE, ITS EXEMPTIONS, AND ITS EXCEPTIONS

PART A. Introduction

§ 10.01 OVERVIEW

The hearsay doctrine is the last major preferential exclusionary doctrine based on doubt about the reliability of a type of evidence. The best evidence rule's underlying rationale is a fear of untrustworthy secondary evidence. The opinion rule expresses the courts' doubts about the reliability of opinions. Underlying the hearsay rule is a fear about the reliability of in-court testimony about out-of-court statements when the proponent is attempting to use the statements as substantive evidence in the case. The common law prefers that the third party (the declarant) appear in court and subject himself or herself to cross-examination. The common law assumes that evidence will be more trustworthy if the declarant testifies under oath, in the jury's view, and subject to cross-examination. The opponent may use cross-examination to expose any errors of perception, memory, narration, or sincerity.

Lay persons commonly think that the hearsay rule applies to any out-of-court statement. In truth, the rule has a relatively narrow scope. Evidence constitutes hearsay only if it is (1) an assertive statement (2) by a human being (3) still considered an out-of-court declarant at the time of trial and (4) offered at trial to prove the truth of the assertion. Federal Rule of Evidence 801 follows this view. The rationale for the rule explains the rule's limited scope. We are interested in the declarant's credibility only when his or her out-of-court statement is being used to prove the truth of the assertion. In that circumstance, the evidence's value depends on the credibility of the out-of-court declarant. For example, suppose that an in-court witness testifies that an out-of-court declarant said that the defendant's car ran a red light. The plaintiff wants to offer the testimony for the purpose of showing that in fact, the defendant's car ran the red light. For that purpose, the testimony's value depends upon the perception and memory of the out-of-court declarant. The opponent thus needs to cross-examine the out-of-court declarant to test the evidence.

However, if the proponent does not offer the out-of-court declaration for its truth, the opponent does not need to cross-examine the declarant. If the declaration is logically relevant on some other theory, the evidence's value usually depends on the credibility of the in-court witness. Suppose that the plaintiff has sued a defendant for slander. The plaintiff alleges that the defendant repeated the slanderous statement to *X*. The plaintiff calls *X*, the in-court witness, to testify that the defendant made an out-of-court statement that the plaintiff bribed a public official. The plaintiff does not want to offer the statement for its truth; quite to the contrary, if the defendant can show that the statement is true, the defendant has a complete defense to tort liability. The plaintiff wants to show only that at a particular time and place the defendant made the slanderous statement. The value of *X*'s testimony depends on *X*'s credibility. Did *X* hear the statement correctly? Does *X* remember the statement correctly? If *X* testifies in court, the defendant can test the value of the evidence. Hence, the limitation on the hearsay rule's scope is a corollary of the rule's rationale; the rule is limited to statements offered to prove their truth because then and only then does the opponent have an acute need to cross-examine the out-of-court declarant.

Even if a statement falls within the definition of hearsay, the statement may be admissible. There are numerous exemptions from and exceptions to the hearsay rule. Federal Rule 801(d) sets out the exemptions for some prior statements and admissions or statements of a party-opponent, Federal Rules 803 and 804 contain a lengthy list of exceptions, and Rule 807 adds a final, residual exception. Part C of this chapter discusses the admission exemption. As that part explains, to bring a statement within the admission exemption, the proponent need not show that the statement was reliable or that there is any necessity for resorting to the statement; all the proponent has to do is to show that the statement should be imputed to the party-opponent. Part D describes a series of hearsay exceptions based primarily on an inference of the reliability of the statement. In contrast, Part E addresses a number of exceptions resting in large part on a showing of necessity; all of these exceptions require proof that the out-of-court declarant is unavailable at the time of trial. Finally, Part F of this chapter describes the residual hearsay exception. To invoke this exception, the proponent must demonstrate both reliability and an element of necessity.

PART B. Hearsay

§ 10.02 THE DEFINITION OF HEARSAY

[1] IN GENERAL

As previously stated, the definition of hearsay is narrow. Federal Rule of Evidence 801(c) states that " '[h]earsay' means a statement that: (1) the declarant does not make while testifying at the current trial or hearing; and (2) a party offers in evidence to prove the truth of the matter asserted in the statement." Rule 801(a) adds that a " '[s]tatement' means a person's oral assertion, written assertion, or nonverbal conduct, if the person intended it as an assertion." Under the Federal Rules, evidence constitutes hearsay only if four conditions are present: (1) the evidence is an assertive statement or act; (2) the assertion was made out of court by a human being; (3) at trial, that person is still considered an out-of-court declarant; and (4) the evidence is being used at trial to prove the truth of the assertion. Evidence falls within the hearsay definition only when all four elements are present; if any element is missing, the evidence is not hearsay, and there is no need to search for a hearsay exception. We shall now examine each of the four elements of the hearsay definition.

[2]   THE EVIDENCE IS AN ASSERTIVE STATEMENT OR ACT

[a]   ASSERTIVE STATEMENTS

All courts agree that assertive statements fall within the hearsay definition. If the person makes an oral out-of-court statement or reduces the statement to writing out of court, the statement could be hearsay. However, it must be remembered that not all statements are assertive. Grammar tells us that there are four types of sentences: declarative, imperative, exclamatory, and interrogatory. As a practical matter, only declarative sentences ordinarily fall within the hearsay definition; they declare or assert facts, including states of mind. Imperative sentences giving orders, exclamatory sentences, and interrogatory sentences posing questions usually fall outside the hearsay definition; if these sentences are relevant at all, it is usually relevant simply that the sentences were uttered, and for that purpose the attorneys can question the person who heard the declarant utter the sentence. There is little or no need to cross-examine the declarant of an imperative, exclamatory, or interrogatory sentence about perception or memory.

If the proponent is going to offer evidence on the theory that it is a non-assertive statement, the foundation usually includes these elements:

1. Where the statement was made.

2. When the statement was made.

3. Who was present.

4. The tenor of the statement.

5. In an offer of proof outside the jury's hearing, the proponent states that the tenor of the statement is nonassertive.

6. In the same offer of proof, the proponent shows that the nonassertive statement is logically relevant to the material facts of consequence in the case.

Our fact situation is a criminal prosecution. The government charges that Messrs. Cetina and Britton conspired to sell and actually sold heroin. The witness is Ms. Grace. Ms. Grace identifies herself. She then testifies that she is a government informant and infiltrated the meeting of a drug ring. The prosecutor is the proponent.

P   Ms. Grace, WHERE were you on the evening of January 17, 2017? (1), (2)

W   I was at 70 Aberdeen Court in downtown Indianapolis.

P   WHO else was there? (3)

W   The two defendants, Cetina and Britton.

P   WHERE are they now? (3)

W   In the courtroom.

P   Specifically, WHERE in the courtroom? (3)

W	At that table over there.
P	HOW are they dressed? (3)
W	Cetina is wearing a blue suit with red tie. Britton has a brown suit and yellow tie.
P	Your Honor, please let the record reflect that the witness has identified the two accused.
J	It will so reflect.
P	Ms. Grace, WHAT happened during this meeting? (4)
W	The accused made some plans.
P	WHAT plans did they discuss? (4)
O	Your Honor, I object to that question on the ground that it calls for incompetent hearsay.
P	Your Honor, may we approach the bench and be heard?
J	Yes.
P	(*Out of the jury's hearing*) Your Honor, I offer to prove that the witness will testify that the accused Cetina ordered the accused Britton to get some bags of heroin out of Britton's car and that Britton did so. (4) Cetina's statement is not hearsay because it is not assertive; the statement is not a declarative sentence but rather an imperative one, ordering Britton to do something. (5) The only thing we're interested in is whether he gave the order. You might say that Ms. Grace is an "earwitness" to the fact that he gave the order. The statement is logically relevant to prove the existence of a conspiracy between them. (6)
J	The objection will be overruled.
P	Ms. Grace, let me repeat the question. WHAT plans did they discuss? (4)
W	The plans for a drug sale. Cetina ordered Britton to get some bags of heroin out of Britton's car to get them ready for sale.
P	WHAT happened then?
W	Britton left for a couple of minutes and then came back with some bags.
P	WHAT was the appearance of the bags?
W	The bags themselves were transparent.
P	WHAT, if anything, could you see in the bags?
W	There was a white, powdery substance in each bag.

In the final analysis, it is always a question of interpretation whether the statement is an assertion. Sometimes an exclamatory, imperative, or interrogatory sentence contains an assertion, and the proponent may be interested only in the assertion. Assume, for instance, that in the above hypothetical, the accused were charged with substantive drug offenses rather than conspiracy and that the only question was whether the bags contained heroin. It is true that overall Cetina's utterance is an imperative sentence: "Go out to your car and get the bags of heroin." However, in this context, the prosecutor would be interested only in the part of the sentence in which Cetina referred to "the bags of heroin." In fact, at trial, rather than questioning Grace about the entire sentence, the prosecutor might ask only: "How did Mr. Cetina describe the bags?" or "What did Mr. Cetina say about the contents of the bags?" Although the overall formal classification of the sentence is imperative, the prosecutor is attempting to elicit an assertion embodied in the sentence; and for that reason, functionally the question calls for hearsay.

[b] ASSERTIVE ACTS

Sometimes a person intends an act to be a true substitute for speech. For instance, persons sometimes nod or shake their heads in response to questions. In principle, these acts should be treated in the same fashion as verbal hearsay statements; these acts present the same probative dangers of perception, memory, narration, and sincerity. For this reason, all courts agree that like assertive statements, assertive acts fall within the hearsay definition. Federal Rule of Evidence 801(a)(2) is illustrative; that rule includes within the hearsay definition "nonverbal conduct of a person, if the person intended it as an assertion." The prevailing view is that the opponent objecting to the admission of the testimony as hearsay has the burden of convincing the judge that the conduct was assertive in nature. If the opponent fails to satisfy that burden, the judge will overrule the hearsay objection.

The following hypothetical illustrates the scope of the hearsay definition. The fact situation is a robbery prosecution. The witness is a police officer. The officer, Patrolman Glancy, has already identified himself. He testifies that he investigated the crime, interviewed the victim, and brought the victim to the police station. Assume that in this jurisdiction, a witness's prior identification of a person is not admissible to bolster the witness's credibility. The proponent is the prosecutor.

P	WHAT happened after you took the victim, Mr. Clayton, to the police station?
W	I talked to him, and then I took him to the lineup room.
P	WHAT is the lineup room?
W	It's the room in the station where we permit victims and eyewitnesses to view suspects. We hope that they can pick the criminal out of the lineup parade.
P	WHAT happened after you took Mr. Clayton into the interview room?
O	Your Honor, I object to that question on the ground that it calls for incompetent hearsay.
P	Your Honor, may we approach the bench and be heard?
J	Yes.
P	Your Honor, the witness is prepared to testify that at the lineup, Mr. Clayton pointed to the accused. The evidence can't be hearsay because

	Mr. Clayton didn't say anything. He just pointed.
O	Mr. Clayton's act of pointing is an assertive act; he subjectively intended it to be a substitute for the verbal statement that the defendant was the robber. Assertive acts fall within the hearsay definition.
J	I agree with the defense counsel. Under Rule 104(a), I find that the act was subjectively intended to be the functional equivalent of an assertive statement. The objection will be sustained.

The prevailing view is that the objecting party has the burden of proving that the statement was subjectively intended as a true substitute for speech and, therefore, constituted hearsay. The Advisory Committee Note to Rule 801(a) commits the federal courts to that view.

[c] NONASSERTIVE ACTS

Although the courts agree that assertive statements and acts are within the hearsay definition, they disagree over a third category of evidence: nonassertive acts. A classic English case, *Wright v. Tatham*, contained this fact situation. The issue was a testator's mental capacity. The proponent of the will was attempting to prove that the testator was mentally competent. To prove that, the proponent offered to show that several persons had written serious business letters to the testator. Although the act of writing the letter incidentally involved assertions in the letters, the act itself was nonassertive; the persons did not subjectively intend their act to substitute for the verbal statement that the testator was competent. However, the authors of the letters assumed that the testator was competent to understand the contents of the letters they sent the testator, and the proponent of the will offered the evidence to show the truth of their assumption and belief. The proponent of the will reasoned that they would not have mailed the testator serious letters unless they believed he was competent; and if they, his close acquaintances, believed him to be competent, he probably was competent. The English court held that the evidence fell within the hearsay definition; the court argued that even though the act was nonassertive, it presented probative dangers of perception and memory. This case was the landmark case for the traditional common-law view that evidence of a nonassertive act is hearsay if (1) the act is apparently actuated or prompted by a certain belief and (2) the proponent offers the evidence to prove the truth of the belief. In 1992, the English House of Lords reaffirmed that *Wright* is still good law in that jurisdiction.

The trend in the American statutes and case law has been to the contrary. If the person is willing to act on his or her belief, the person's willingness removes most doubts about the person's sincerity; and there is much less justification for including the evidence within the hearsay rule. Federal Rule of Evidence 801 excludes this evidence, sometimes called Morgan hearsay, from its hearsay definition. The Advisory Committee took the position that the dangers of this type of evidence are "minimal in the absence of an intent to assert and do not justify the loss of the evidence on hearsay grounds."

The following hypothetical illustrates the third category of evidence. We can adapt the basic fact situation in *Wright*. The testator is the decedent, Mr. Marsden. The decedent owned a large car dealership. The proponent of the will is Mr. Wright. Mr. Wright calls Mr. Toscher as a witness. Mr. Toscher owns a janitorial services company. Mr. Wright wants to show that Toscher sent Mr. Marsden a serious business proposal for janitorial services on the decedent's car lot. During closing argument, Mr. Wright's attorney wants to use Toscher's conduct as evidence of Mr. Marsden's competency: Toscher would not have sent Marsden the letter unless he, Toscher, believed that Marsden was mentally competent. Mr. Toscher has already identified himself and stated his line of business.

P	WHERE were you on the morning of April 16, 2017?
W	In my office in downtown Kansas City.
P	WHAT were you doing there?
W	I was getting some bids ready on some new contracts for janitorial services.
P	WHAT is a bid?
W	We offer services to a company at a certain monthly rate. Then they decide whether they want to award the work to us or another company.
P	WHAT did you do after you finished the bids?
W	I mailed them.
P	WHOM did you mail them to?
W	Several people, including the decedent, Mr. Marsden.
O	Your Honor, I move to strike the last question and answer on the ground that they are irrelevant.
P	Your Honor, may we approach the bench?
J	Yes.
P	Your Honor, the evidence shows that Mr. Toscher mailed a serious business proposal to Mr. Marsden. That conduct shows Mr. Toscher's belief in Mr. Marsden's mental competency; he wouldn't have mailed him that sort of letter unless he thought Mr. Marsden was competent.
O	Now I object on the ground that the evidence is hearsay.
P	How can it be hearsay if it's evidence of a nonassertive act?
O	Your Honor, as you know, this jurisdiction subscribes to the traditional view that even a nonassertive act is hearsay if (1) it's actuated by a belief and (2) it's used to prove the truth of the belief. The opposing counsel has shown he's really interested in Mr. Toscher's belief in Mr. Marsden's competency, and the counsel wants to use the belief as evidence of Marsden's competency.
J	The objection will be sustained.

Assume that this case arose in a jurisdiction following the modern view that nonassertive acts fall outside the hearsay definition. The proper objection would be that the proponent has not laid a proper foundation for skilled lay observer opinion testimony. On the witness stand, a lay person may not express an opinion of another person's sanity unless he or she is intimately familiar with that person. Change the judge's hearsay ruling and continue the hypothetical.

J	Counsel, you overlook the fact that this jurisdiction recently adopted the Federal Rules, excluding nonassertive acts from the hearsay definition.
O	Very well, Your Honor. My other objection is that the proponent hasn't shown that the witness knew Mr. Marsden well enough to express an opinion about Marsden's competency. Your Honor, if you admit this evidence, you are in effect permitting Toscher to give skilled lay observer opinion testimony about Marsden's competency or sanity. I request permission to take the witness on voir dire.
J	Permission granted.
O	Mr. Toscher, ISN'T IT TRUE THAT you never personally met the decedent, Mr. Marsden?
W	Yes.
O	ISN'T IT A FACT THAT the only letters you ever received from his company were signed by other persons?
W	Yes.
O	ISN'T IT CORRECT THAT you never had a telephone conversation with Mr. Marsden?
W	Yes.
O	ISN'T IT TRUE THAT your only information about Mr. Marsden is what other people told you about him?
W	Yes.
O	Your Honor, I have no further voir dire questions of this witness. I renew my objection that the question calls for improper lay opinion testimony.
J	The objection will be sustained. The foundation doesn't satisfy Rule 701.

[3]   THE STATEMENT IS OFFERED FOR A HEARSAY PURPOSE

[a]   OVERVIEW

Even if the statement is assertive, the statement is not hearsay under Rule 801(c)(2) unless the proponent offers the statement to prove the truth of the assertion. Offering the statement for that purpose creates the need to cross-examine the declarant about perception or memory. This step in hearsay analysis parallels the second step in best evidence analysis: Just as the best evidence rule does not come into play unless the writing's terms are in issue, a statement is not hearsay unless the proponent offers the statement to prove the truth of an assertion contained in the statement. The statement is deemed hearsay only when the immediate inference the proponent wants to draw is the truth of the assertion on the statement's face. If the proponent can demonstrate that the statement is logically relevant on any other theory, the statement is nonhearsay. When the proponent offers the statement for a nonhearsay purpose, we are primarily interested simply in the fact that the statement was made. The fact *of* the statement is relevant; the truth of the facts *in* the statement is irrelevant. The only need to cross-examine is the need to question on the stand the witness who heard the statement made.

When the proponent is going to argue a nonhearsay theory for admitting a statement, the foundation includes these elements:

1. Where the statement was made.

2. When the statement was made.

3. Who was present.

4. The tenor of the statement.

5. In an offer of proof, the proponent states that he or she intends to use the statement for a nonhearsay purpose.

6. In the same offer of proof, the proponent shows that on that nonhearsay theory, the statement is logically relevant.

There are three common nonhearsay uses of evidence. First, the proponent may argue that the statement is circumstantial evidence of the declarant's state of mind. If the declarant's state of mind is logically relevant in the case, the proponent may use the declarant's statements as circumstantial proof of such states of mind as malice, hatred, premeditation, and love. Sometimes the mere fact that a person makes a certain statement gives us valuable insight into that person's frame of mind. Second, the statement may be an operative fact or verbal act in the case. In some situations, legal consequences flow directly from the use of certain words such as the offer in a contract suit or the slander in a tort action. Written contracts typically contain many assertive sentences, but given the objective theory of mutual assent the contracts are admissible as nonhearsay. This theory is applicable to commercial instruments such as promissory notes and mortgages. Again the mere fact that the declarant uttered the words is logically relevant; under substantive law, the words themselves have legal consequences. Finally, the proponent can prove the statement to show its effect on the state of mind of the hearer or reader. For example, if it is disputed whether the defendant knew of a certain dangerous condition, it is logically relevant to prove that someone told him of the condition. Quite apart from the truth of the third party's statement, the statement puts the defendant on notice. The following hypotheticals illustrate these various nonhearsay uses.

[b]   THE STATEMENT IS CIRCUMSTANTIAL PROOF OF THE DECLARANT'S STATE OF MIND—MENTAL OUTPUT

Our fact situation is a dispute over title to real property. The decedent, Joan Furlow, formerly owned the land. Before she died, she gave her nephew, Garrett Furlow, a deed to the property; she gave him the deed on April 14, 2017. The executor claims that although Ms. Furlow gave Garrett the deed, she did not intend the deed to be immediately effective; and since she did not have the intent required by Real Property law, the deed was ineffective. The nephew calls Ms. Barbara Peterson as a witness. Ms. Peterson identifies herself and states that she knew the decedent for several years. The nephew is the proponent.

P	WHERE were you on April 13, 2017? (1), (2)
W	I was visiting Joan at her house on Dwight Street.
P	WHO else was there? (3)
W	Only the two of us.
P	WHAT happened while you were there? (4)
W	We just had a nice chat.
P	WHAT did you chat about? (4)
W	A lot of things, including Joan's nephew, Garrett.
P	WHAT did Ms. Furlow say about her nephew, Garrett? (4)
O	Your Honor, I object to that question on the ground that it calls for hearsay.
P	Your Honor, may we approach the bench?
J	Yes.
P	Your Honor, I offer to prove that Ms. Peterson will testify that Ms. Furlow said that her nephew was a man in a million. (4) Ms. Furlow may have been mistaken in thinking that her nephew was a man in a million, but that is beside the point. I want to offer that testimony for a nonhearsay purpose, as circumstantial proof of Ms. Furlow's affection for Garrett. (5) The testimony is logically relevant to show that she had donative intent when she gave him the deed the next day. (6)
J	The objection will be overruled. I will admit the evidence for that nonhearsay purpose.
P	Ms. Peterson, let me repeat the question. WHAT did Ms. Furlow say about her nephew, Garrett? (4)
W	She said that he was a man in a million.
O	Your Honor, I request a limiting instruction under Rule 105.
J	Yes. Ladies and gentlemen of the jury, you have just heard Ms. Peterson's testimony about Ms. Furlow's statement. I am admitting the evidence of Ms. Furlow's statement only for the purpose of showing Ms. Furlow's state of mind, her feeling or affection for her nephew.

Given the trial judge's limiting instruction, during closing argument the proponent's attorney could legitimately use the testimony about the decedent's statement to prove her donative intent: "Ladies and gentlemen, in her instructions your Honor is going to tell you that we need to prove that on April 14, 2017, when Ms. Furlow handed Garrett the deed to the house on Dwight Street, she actually intended to make a gift to Garrett. Think back to Ms. Peterson's testimony. She told you that on April 13th—one day before—Ms. Furlow told her that Garrett was a man in a million. Obviously, you don't have to decide whether Garrett is one man in a million. However, the fact that Ms. Furlow said that the day before tells you how much affection she had for her nephew Garrett—such strong affection and love that she wanted him to have the property on Dwight Street."

[c]   THE STATEMENT IS AN OPERATIVE FACT OR VERBAL ACT

To illustrate this foundation, we shall use a variation of the fact situation in *Hanson v. Johnson*, 161 Minn. 229, 201 N.W. 322 (1924). In that case, the plaintiff Hanson owned a farm that he leased to Schrik. There were a number of large cribs on the farm for storing corn, and Schrik intended to use the farm to raise corn. In our variation of the fact situation, Schrik falls behind in his rent. He then enters into an agreement with Hanson. Under the agreement, Hanson will accept the corn stored in two cribs, five and seven, in lieu of rent due for June and July. When they enter into the agreement at the farm, Schrik says: "It's a deal. The corn in cribs five and seven is yours." Later Schrik obtains a loan from Cattlemen's Bank. He pledges "my corn" as security for the loan. He defaults on the loan. The bank forecloses and sells all the corn on the premises, including the corn in cribs five and seven. Hanson then sues the bank for conversion. Hanson is the witness. He has already identified himself, explained that he was Schrik's landlord, and testifies that Schrik was delinquent on his rent. The plaintiff is the proponent.

P	Mr. Hanson, WHERE were you on the afternoon of July 6, 2017? (1), (2)
W	I was at the farm, the one I rented to Schrik.
P	WHO else was there? (3)
W	Schrik was the only one around. I didn't see his wife or kids.
P	WHY were you there? (4)
W	As I said, he'd fallen behind in his rent. He was supposed to pay at the beginning of the month, and he'd missed the June and July payments. I asked him what he intended to do about the delinquent rent.
P	WHAT happened when you asked him that? (4)
W	He offered me a deal.
O	Your Honor, I move to strike that last answer on the ground that it is hearsay.
P	Your Honor, may we approach the bench?
J	Yes.
P	Your Honor, I offer to prove that Mr. Hanson will testify that Mr. Schrik offered to give my client the corn in two cribs, cribs five and seven, in exchange for the delinquent rent. (4) I want to use the statement for a nonhearsay purpose, namely, to show the offer itself. (5) The words constituting the offer for the contract are an operative fact or verbal act; in Contract law, legal consequences flow directly from the fact that

Schrik uttered those words. (6)

J	The motion will be denied.
P	Mr. Hanson, let me repeat the question. WHAT happened when you asked him about the delinquent rent? (4)
W	He offered to give me the corn in two cribs in exchange for the late rent.
P	WHAT were his words? (4)
W	As best I recall, he said, "It's a deal. The corn in cribs five and seven is yours."
P	WHAT did you say then? (4)
W	I just said that I accepted the offer, and we shook on it.

[d] THE EFFECT OF THE STATEMENT ON THE MIND OF THE HEARER OR READER—MENTAL INPUT

Suppose that the plaintiff, Zillman, alleged that the defendant has been negligent in two respects. First, the defendant was speeding. Second, the defendant carelessly drove the car although he knew that the car had bad brakes. Under the second theory, one issue would be whether the defendant knew that the brakes were defective. The plaintiff calls Mr. John Horne. Horne testifies that he manages the auto repair shop near the defendant's house. Horne adds that on January 14, 2016, the defendant dropped off his car for regular maintenance. The plaintiff is the proponent.

P	Mr. Horne, WHERE were you on January 16, 2016? (1), (2)
W	I was at my repair shop.
P	WHO else was there? (3)
W	We had several customers, including the defendant.
P	WHAT happened when the defendant came into the shop? (4)
W	He was there to pick up his car.
P	WHAT happened while he was there? (4)
W	He got the car, and we talked for a while.
P	WHAT did you talk about? (4)
W	Mostly his car.
P	WHAT did you tell him about the car? (4)
O	Your Honor, I object to that question on the ground that it calls for hearsay.
P	Your Honor, may we approach the bench?
J	Yes.
P	Your Honor, I offer to prove that the witness will testify that he told the defendant his brakes were bad. (4) I want to use the witness's prior statement for a nonhearsay purpose, namely, to show its effect on the

defendant's state of mind; it gave him knowledge and put him on notice that his brakes were bad. (5) Under our second cause of action, this evidence is logically relevant; our second cause is that the defendant negligently drove the car when he knew it had defective brakes. (6)

J   The objection will be overruled.

P   Mr. Horne, let me repeat the question. WHAT did you tell the defendant about his car? (4)

W   I told him that the brakes were bad and could go out any time.

P   HOW close were you standing to the defendant when you told him that?

W   Only a foot or two away.

P   HOW noisy was the repair shop at the time?

W   It was very quiet.

P   HOW were you facing when you told him about his brakes?

W   I was talking right at him.

P   WHO else was talking to him at the time?

W   No one else. We were the only two talking.

P   HOW did he react when you told him about the bad brakes?

W   He nodded his head, shrugged his shoulders, and got into his car.

O   Your Honor, I request a limiting instruction under Rule 105.

J   Yes. Ladies and gentlemen of the jury, you have just heard the witness's testimony that he told the defendant that the defendant's brakes were bad. You may not consider the witness's testimony as evidence that in fact, the brakes were bad. You may consider the witness's testimony only in deciding whether the next day, the defendant knew the car was defective and acted negligently in driving the car. If other evidence in this case establishes that the brakes were bad, then and only then may you consider the witness's testimony—and then only in deciding whether the next day, the defendant knew the brakes were bad and acted negligently in driving the car.

Of course, to sustain the burden of going forward and defeat a directed verdict motion, the proponent will have to introduce other, substantive evidence that the brakes were defective. The plaintiff could call the repairman who actually worked on the brakes to describe the condition of the brakes. However, the plaintiff could use Mr. Horne's testimony for the limited, nonhearsay purpose of proving that the defendant knew of the brakes' hazardous condition. Thus, in closing argument, the plaintiff's attorney might state: "In his instructions to you, his Honor will tell you that we have the burden of proving that before the collision, the defendant knew that his brakes were bad. Ladies and gentlemen, we've proven that. Remember the testimony by Mr. Horne, the owner of the repair shop that the defendant took his car to. Mr. Horne told you that on January 16th—several days before the accident—he had a conversation with the defendant. Mr. Horne added that in that conversation, he told the defendant point blank that the defendant's brakes were bad and could go out at any time. When the defendant drove away from Mr. Horne's shop, the defendant knew good and well that his brakes were defective."

[4]   THE STATEMENT WAS NOT MADE BY A HUMAN DECLARANT

Federal Rule of Evidence 801(a) defines a statement as an assertion by "a person[]." In turn, Rule 801(b) states that a declarant is "the person who made the statement." Those definitions explain why the hearsay rule applies to computer-stored statements but not to computer-generated statements.

Suppose that a business employee inputs data about a sale into a company computer. The input amounts to a statement by a human declarant, the employee. It is true that the statement is stored on the computer hard drive in electronic form. Yet, in the final analysis, the accuracy of the statement depends on the testimonial qualities of the human declarant who was the source of the input. If the company later prints out that data and at trial a litigant offers the printout as proof of the truth of the data, the printout constitutes hearsay; and the proponent will need to lay a foundation for a hearsay exception such as the business entry provision codified in Rule 803(6).

Distinguish a statement generated by an instrument. For instance, assume that the defendant is standing trial on a charge of driving while intoxicated. The prosecutor calls a police officer who administered an intoxilyzer test to the defendant. The officer is prepared to testify that when she administered a test to the defendant, the instrument displayed "0.17." That display is elliptical; it amounts to the assertive statement that the blood alcohol concentration of the person who just blew into the instrument is 0.17. That statement is assertive. Moreover, the prosecution certainly wants to offer the evidence to prove the truth of the assertion. However, the statement was not made by a person under Rule 801(b). The statement was generated by a mechanical instrument. As § 10.01 pointed out, the primary rationale for the hearsay rule is that it safeguards the right to cross-examination. Although it makes sense to give the opposing attorney an opportunity to cross-examine a human declarant, the attorney cannot cross-examine an intoxilyzer. Consequently, the defense could not successfully object on hearsay grounds to the introduction of the testimony about the readout.

Although the hearsay rule is inapplicable to computer-generated statements, there is a validation problem under *Daubert v. Merrell Dow Pharms.*, 509 U.S. 579, 113 S. Ct. 2786, 125 L. Ed. 2d 469 (1993). To generate "0.17," the instrument relied on formulae and scientific propositions embedded in the source code of its software. Those formulae and propositions determine the accuracy of the assertion that the defendant's blood alcohol concentration was 0.17. The proponent of the testimony must establish either that those propositions are judicially noticeable under Federal Rule of Evidence 201(b) or that they qualify as reliable "scientific . . . knowledge" within the meaning of that expression in Rule 702.

Suppose that in a drunk driving prosecution, the government has called a state trooper to testify that when she administered an intoxilyzer test to the defendant, the instrument displayed "0.17." The defense objected on both scientific evidence and hearsay grounds. The trial judge has already overruled the former objection. The prosecutor is the proponent.

J   The first objection will be overruled. As I recall, though, you objected on alternative grounds. Correct?

O   Yes, Your Honor. I also objected on hearsay grounds. "0.17" is shorthand for an assertion—the assertion that my client's blood alcohol concentration was 0.17%. That's clearly a statement under Rule 801(a).

J   Ms. Prosecutor, do you have any response? That statement certainly strikes me as being assertive.

P   Your Honor, I agree it's assertive, but it's still not hearsay. To be hearsay, it not only has to be an assertive statement, it has to come from a hearsay declarant. You have to interpret Rule 801(a) in the light and context of Rule 801(b). Rule 801(b) expressly states that a declarant must be a "person."

O   But, Your Honor, someone programmed the formulae that generated "0.17" into the intoxilyzer. We should be entitled to cross-examine that person before you admit this testimony.

P   Your Honor, you've already ruled that all those formulae are either judicially noticeable or satisfy *Daubert*. This isn't computer-stored information. This isn't a case in which a human being prepared a report and stored the report in a computer. In contrast, this is computer-generated data. The accuracy of "0.17" doesn't depend on the credibility of any human being; it depends on the validity of the formulae, and you've already overruled the defense's first objection. It's well-settled that computer-generated data is not hearsay.

J   I agree. The second objection will also be overruled. You may proceed.

[5] THE STATEMENT WAS MADE OR THE ACT PERFORMED BY A PERSON STILL CONSIDERED AN OUT-OF-COURT DECLARANT

Assume that the proponent is offering testimony about a human declarant's out-of-court statement for the truth of the assertion. Offering the evidence for that purpose creates an acute need to cross-examine the declarant about his or her perception, memory, and other testimonial qualities. However, suppose that the declarant becomes a witness at trial. If so, the opposing attorney can cross-examine the person both about the person's in-court testimony and about the earlier statements. The person's current availability seemingly satisfies the need for cross-examination. Does the person's current availability for cross-examination remove the earlier statements from the definition of hearsay?

The traditional view is "once an out-of-court declarant, always an out-of-court declarant." If the person was not on the stand when he or she made the statement, it is immaterial that the person later becomes a witness and subjects himself or herself to cross-examination. Consider this example. On Monday, the person tells a friend that the person saw the defendant's car run the red light. On Tuesday, that same person becomes a witness in the suit between plaintiff and defendant. The person testifies that he or she saw the defendant's car run the red light. To increase the impact of the testimony, the plaintiff's attorney attempts to elicit the person's testimony that Monday the person told the friend the same story. If the proponent attempts to use the statement on Monday as substantive proof of the defendant's fault, the statement is hearsay; although the person is now the witness, the person was not on the witness stand when the person made the statement. Under the traditional view—"once a hearsay declarant, always a hearsay declarant"—the hearsay rule would apply even if the person made the statement on the courthouse steps ten minutes before taking the witness stand.

Several commentators, including Morgan, argued that the definition of hearsay should not include prior statements made by witnesses now on the stand and subject to cross-examination. These commentators begin with the premise that the primary purpose of the hearsay rule is to protect the opponent's right to cross-examine. They then argue that the opportunity to cross-examine is adequate even if the opportunity is delayed until trial; on Tuesday, the opponent can cross-examine the witness about Monday's statement. These commentators conclude that if the person is now a witness available for examination in court, the person should no longer be considered an out-of-court declarant; and the hearsay rule should not apply to the witness's prior statements. To date, only one jurisdiction, Kansas, has formally adopted this view, although several older Georgia opinions also contain broad language seemingly endorsing this view.

There is a compromise view gaining a growing number of adherents. The compromise view is that if the witness's prior statement is otherwise admissible for a nonhearsay purpose (as a prior identification to bolster, as a prior inconsistent statement to impeach, or as a prior consistent statement to rehabilitate), the statement should be admitted as substantive evidence. Federal Rules of Evidence partially embrace the compromise view. Rule 801(d)(1) exempts certain prior statements of the witness from the hearsay definition and permits their use as substantive evidence: "A statement that meets the following conditions is not hearsay: (1) A Declarant-Witness's Prior Statement. The declarant testifies and is subject to cross-examination about a prior statement, and the statement: (A) is inconsistent with the declarant's testimony and was given under penalty of perjury at a trial, hearing, or other proceeding or in a deposition; (B) is consistent with the declarant's testimony and is offered: (i) to rebut an express or implied charge that the declarant recently fabricated it or acted from a recent improper influence or motive in so testifying or (ii) to rehabilitate the declarant's credibility as a witness when attacked on another ground; or (C) identifies a person as someone the declarant perceived earlier." This compromise view reflects two beliefs. First, its supporters believe that there is substantial merit in Morgan's position. Second, they frankly suspect that limiting instructions are largely ineffective; although the judge tells the jurors to use the prior statement for the limited purpose of bolstering, impeaching, or rehabilitating, many jurors will misuse the statement and treat it as substantive evidence of the assertion. These two beliefs lead the supporters of the compromise view to admit prior statements as substantive evidence when the statements are otherwise admissible, usually on one of the credibility theories discussed in Chapter 5.

In a jurisdiction wholeheartedly embracing Morgan's view, the foundation for the prior statement is simple. The foundation includes these elements:

1.   Where the prior statement was made.

2.   When the statement was made.

3.   Who was present.

4.   The present witness made the prior statement.

5.   The tenor of the statement.

The fact situation is a tort action arising from a collision. The plaintiff, Mr. Kionka, contends that on January 17, 2017, the defendant caused the accident by speeding. Mr. Kionka calls Ms. Gerst as a witness. She identifies herself, states that she observed the two cars, and expresses her opinion that defendant's car was going 60 miles an hour. Her direct examination continues. The proponent is the plaintiff.

P	WHERE were you on January 18, 2017? (1), (2)
W	I went down to the police station on Mission Boulevard.
P	WHY did you go there?
W	The officer at the accident scene told me to stop by and give a statement the next day.
P	WHAT happened when you arrived at the police station? (3)
W	I met Officer Grouton, the traffic sergeant.
P	WHAT, if anything, did you tell him about the accident? (4), (5)
O	Your Honor, I object to that question on the ground that it calls for hearsay.
P	Your Honor, may we approach the bench?
J	Yes.
P	Your Honor, the witness is present in court and available for cross-examination. In this jurisdiction, in that situation, the witness's prior statements are no longer considered hearsay.
J	Correct. The objection will be overruled.
P	Ms. Gerst, let me repeat the question. WHAT, if anything, did you tell Officer Grouton about the accident? (4), (5)
W	I said I thought the defendant caused the accident because he was speeding about 60 miles an hour.

In a jurisdiction following the compromise view, the proponent would have to show that the prior statement is admissible on a nonhearsay theory. The proponent would have to lay a complete foundation for prior identification, prior inconsistent statement, or prior consistent statement. Chapter 5 outlines those foundations. Suppose that on February 14, 2017, Ms. Gerst told a friend that she thought the defendant was going only 40 miles an hour. In a compromise jurisdiction, the defendant could use Ms. Gerst's prior inconsistent statement as substantive evidence; no limiting instruction would be given. The hypothetical continues, and the defendant now attempts to prove the prior inconsistent statement during Ms. Gerst's cross-examination. The defendant is the proponent.

P	ISN'T IT A FACT THAT on February 14, 2017, you had a conversation with your friend, Charles Gill, at your house?
W	Yes.
P	ISN'T IT CORRECT THAT during the conversation, you told him that the defendant was going only 40 miles an hour?
W	Yes.
O	Your Honor, I request a limiting instruction.
J	What type of limiting instruction?
O	An instruction that the jurors may consider Ms. Gerst's statement only in so far as it reflects on her credibility.
P	Your Honor, may we approach the bench?
J	Yes.
P	Your Honor, a limiting instruction would be inappropriate.
O	The defendant is obviously introducing this statement as a prior inconsistent statement to impeach; it can't be used as substantive evidence of the defendant's speed.
P	Your Honor, in our jurisdiction, if a witness's prior statement is admissible for a nonhearsay purpose such as impeachment and the witness is available for cross-examination, the hearsay rule no longer applies. Since Ms. Gerst is available for cross-examination, I can use her prior inconsistent statement both to impeach and as substantive evidence.
J	I agree. I shall not give the jurors a limiting instruction.

Note that Federal Rule of Evidence 801(d)(1)(A) stops short of wholeheartedly embracing the compromise view. Under that subsection, it is not enough that the statement be otherwise admissible as a prior inconsistent statement. To ensure that the statute would not violate the confrontation clause, Congress wrote into the statute the additional requirement that the statement had been made both under oath and at a prior formal proceeding such as a grand jury hearing. In short, even if a statement qualifies as a prior inconsistent statement under Rule 613, the statement might not be admissible as substantive evidence under Rule 801(d)(1)(A).

Moreover, in *Tome v. United States*, 513 U.S. 150, 115 S. Ct. 696, 130 L. Ed. 2d 574 (1995), the United States Supreme Court ruled that, at least when a prior consistent statement is offered as substantive evidence, the statement must antedate any improper motive. In effect, the Court held that Rule 801(d)(1)(B) incorporates the common-law temporal priority doctrine. At the time of the writing of the prior edition, 801(d)(1)(B) required that the consistent statement be offered "to rebut an express or implied charge that the declarant recently fabricated [his or her testimony] or acted from a recent improper influence or motive in so testifying." However, the Supreme Court approved an amendment to (d)(1)(B) extending the provision to consistent statements offered "to rehabilitate the declarant's credibility as a witness when attacked on another ground." The amendment took effect on December 1, 2014. The accompanying Advisory Committee Note states that "[t]he intent of the amendment is to extend substantive effect to consistent statements that rebut other attacks on a witness—such as charges of inconsistency or faulty memory."

PART C. The Admissions Exemption Requiring a Showing of Neither Reliability Nor Necessity

§ 10.03 THE EXEMPTION FOR STATEMENTS OR ADMISSIONS OF A PARTY-OPPONENT

[1] IN GENERAL

If the statement falls within the definition of hearsay, the proponent of the statement must find an applicable hearsay exemption or exception. One of the most frequently used exemptions is that for the statements or admissions of a party-opponent. For example, in a tort action the plaintiff can prove the defendant's out-of-court statements acknowledging fault. From the plaintiff's perspective, the defendant's statements are admissions of the party-opponent. The same hearsay exemption permits prosecutors to introduce accused's confessions acknowledging guilt.

Although the common law treats the admission doctrine as a hearsay exception, the admission doctrine differs from most hearsay exceptions. Commentators have had some difficulty explaining the admission doctrine. Unlike most hearsay exceptions, admissions do not have to have a circumstantial guarantee of trustworthiness; although the admission is obviously disserving at the time of trial, the admission is admissible even if it was self-serving when made. Nor is there any need to show a necessity for resorting to the hearsay; the opposing party may be available and perfectly willing to testify about the subject-matter of the earlier statement. The truth of the matter is that like the word product doctrine, the admission doctrine is a product of the adversary litigation system; the opponent can hardly complain that he or she does not have an opportunity to cross-examine himself or herself. The opponent can always take the stand to deny or explain the statement. Because of the unique rationale for this exception, some commentators do not even classify admissions as hearsay. Thus, Federal Rule of Evidence 801(d)(2) exempts admissions from the hearsay definition and admits admissions as "not hearsay." The restyled Rules effect a second change from the common law; the new Rules use the expression, "an opposing party's statement," rather than the traditional terminology "admission."

Although the commentators and courts disagree over the question whether admissions should be classified as hearsay, there is general consensus on the foundational elements of the various types of admissions. There are three basic kinds of admissions: personal, adoptive, and vicarious. The basis of the classification is the reason for which we attribute the statement to the party-opponent. In the case of personal admissions, we attribute the statement to the party-opponent because we find the statement in the party's own words or acts. In the case of adoptive admissions, a third party makes the statement, but we impute the statement to the party-opponent because the opponent manifests agreement with the assertion in the statement. The opponent thereby "adopts" the statement. Finally, in the case of vicarious admissions, again a third party makes the statement, but the party-opponent does not manifest agreement. Instead, we attribute the statement to the party-opponent because of a close legal relationship, such as agency, between the third party and the party-opponent. We shall now examine the foundations for these various types of admissions in detail.

[2]   PERSONAL ADMISSIONS

[a]   OVERVIEW

All jurisdictions admit the party-opponent's own personal admissions in civil and criminal cases. Federal Rule of Evidence 801(d)(2)(A) sanctions the admission of personal admissions. It permits the proponent to introduce a statement when "(t)he statement is offered against an opposing party and . . . was made by the party in an individual or representative capacity." Personal admissions are liberally admissible; the phrasing of the admission can be highly opinionated, and the admission need not even be based on personal knowledge.

[b]   IN CIVIL CASES

In civil cases, the foundation for personal admissions is very simple. The foundation includes these elements:

1.   The witness heard a declarant make a statement.

2.   The witness identifies the declarant as the present party-opponent.

3.   The statement is inconsistent with the position the party-opponent is taking at trial. (Although the appellate courts often phrase this requirement negatively and seem to insist upon inconsistency, in practice trial judges apply the requirement affirmatively; trial judges ask whether the statement is logically relevant under Rule 401 to an issue the proponent has a right to prove in the case. The phrasing of the question eliciting the statement usually ensures the statement's logical relevance; the question inquires "about" a specific topic.)

Our fact situation is a civil tort action. The case arose from a collision on May 19, 2017. The plaintiff, Ms. Langdale, alleges that the defendant, Mr. Maire, caused the collision by speeding. The speed limit in this section of town is 25 miles an hour. The plaintiff calls the investigating officer, Patrolman Hightower. The witness has already identified himself and testified that he went to the accident scene. The proponent is the plaintiff.

P   WHAT did you do when you arrived at the scene of the collision?

W   I investigated the accident.

P   HOW did you investigate the accident? (1)

W   I viewed the debris and interviewed the persons involved.

P	WHOM did you interview? (2)
W	Ms. Langdale and Mr. Maire.
P	WHERE is Mr. Maire now? (2)
W	In the courtroom.
P	Specifically, WHERE in the courtroom? (2)
W	He's sitting at the table.
P	HOW is he dressed? (2)
W	In a green suit and blue tie.
P	Your Honor, please let the record reflect that the witness has identified the defendant.
J	It will so reflect.
P	Officer Hightower, WHAT did the defendant say about the accident? (3)
O	Your Honor, I object on the ground that the question calls for hearsay.
P	Your Honor, may I be heard?
J	Yes.
P	The statement is hearsay, but it falls within the exception for admissions of a party-opponent.
	(In federal court, the proponent would say, "The statement is exempt from the hearsay rule because it is the statement or admission of a party-opponent" or "The statement is not hearsay because it is the statement or admission of a party-opponent.")
J	The objection will be overruled.
P	Let me repeat the question. WHAT did the defendant say about the accident? (3)
W	He said he was really sorry about it because he thought he caused it by going too fast.
P	HOW fast did he say he was going? (3)
W	He said maybe 40 miles an hour.

[c] IN CRIMINAL CASES

The foundation for a criminal accused's confession is more complex than the foundation for admissions in civil cases. The foundation is more complex because in a criminal case, the prosecutor must comply with constitutional requirements as well as common-law hearsay requirements. The prosecutor must first demonstrate that the confession was voluntary; the Fifth and Fourteenth amendment due process clauses bar the admission of involuntary confessions. Furthermore, if the accused was in custody, the prosecutor must demonstrate that the police administered proper *Miranda* warnings; *Miranda* imposes requirements in addition to traditional voluntariness. Finally, the prosecutor must prove that the accused properly waived his or her *Miranda* rights. In

2000, in *Dickerson v. United States*, 530 U.S. 428, 120 S. Ct. 2326, 147 L. Ed. 2d 405 (2000), the Supreme Court affirmed that *Miranda* is still good law. Thus, the complete foundation includes these elements:

1. The witness heard a declarant make a statement.

2. The witness identifies the declarant as the present accused.

3. Any confession was voluntary.

4. The police administered proper *Miranda* warnings to the accused.

5. The accused waived his or her rights.

6. The statement is inconsistent with the position the accused takes at trial; the statement is logically relevant to some issue the prosecution has a right to prove at trial. If the accused pleads not guilty, the accused defendant requires the prosecution to prove all the elements of the crime. By pleading not guilty, the defendant takes the general position that all the facts alleged are false.

Our fact situation is a prosecution for robbery. The accused is Mr. Walters. The prosecution calls Officer Gannon as a witness. Officer Gannon identifies himself and then testifies that he is assigned to the robbery detail of the Lincoln, Nebraska Police Department. The proponent is the prosecutor.

P	Officer Gannon, WHERE were you on the afternoon of January 20, 2017?
W	I was at our downtown station on duty in the robbery detail office.
P	WHAT happened that afternoon?
W	Some other officers brought in someone for questioning.
P	WHO was that person? (2)
W	James Walters.
P	WHERE is James Walters now? (2)
W	Here in the courtroom.
P	Specifically WHERE in the courtroom? (2)
W	He's sitting right there.
P	HOW is he dressed? (2)
W	He's attired in a brown shirt and green pants.
P	Your Honor, please let the record reflect that the witness identified the accused.
J	It will so reflect.
P	WHAT happened after the officers brought Mr. Walters in? (3)
W	I took him to the interrogation room.
P	WHAT happened then? (3)
W	I began questioning him.

P	WHAT promises, if any, did you make to him during the questioning? (3)
W	None.
P	WHAT force, if any, did you use during the interrogation? (3)
W	None. I never touched him.
P	WHAT threats, if any, did you make? (3)
W	I didn't make any. I didn't threaten him or his family in any way.
P	WHAT requests, if any, did he make during the questioning? (3)
W	He asked for a cigarette, for coffee, and to go to the bathroom—that sort of thing.
P	HOW did you respond to his requests? (3)
W	I granted them. I gave him cigarettes and coffee. I let him go to the bathroom. I tried to make him as comfortable as possible.
P	WHAT, if anything, did you say to Mr. Walters? (4)
W	I read him his rights.
P	HOW did you read him his rights? (4)
W	I read them verbatim from a warning card.
P	Your Honor, I request that this be marked prosecution exhibit number three for identification.
J	It will be so marked.
P	Please let the record reflect that I am showing the exhibit to the opposing counsel.
J	It will so reflect.
P	I request permission to approach the witness.
J	Permission granted.
P	Officer Gannon, I now hand you prosecution exhibit number three for identification. WHAT is it? (4)
W	It's the warning card I just referred to.
P	HOW can you recognize it? (4)
W	I initialed it, and I had the defendant initial it as well. I see the initials and the date we wrote in pencil on the card.
P	HOW did you use the card during the questioning? (3)
W	I read from it verbatim to make certain I gave the suspect the correct warnings.
P	Your Honor, I now offer prosecution exhibit number three for identification into evidence as prosecution exhibit three.

J	It will be received.
P	Officer Gannon, please read prosecution exhibit three.
W	It says: "You have a right to remain silent. Anything you say can and will be used against you in a court of law. You also have a right to an attorney. You have a right to consult an attorney before any questioning. You have a right to have an attorney present during any questioning. If you cannot afford an attorney, one will be appointed to represent you."
P	WHAT happened after you read Mr. Walters these rights? (5)
W	I asked him whether he understood his rights.
P	WHAT was his answer? (5)
W	He said he did.
P	WHAT happened then? (5)
W	I asked him whether he wanted an attorney.
P	WHAT was his response?
W	He said no.
P	WHAT happened then? (5)
W	I asked him whether he was willing to talk about the robbery.
P	WHAT was his response? (5)
W	He told me about the robbery.
P	WHAT did he say about the robbery? (6)
W	He said he had held up the McDonald's on 4th Street, and he was very sorry he had done it. He said he needed money for rent, and he couldn't figure out any other way to get it.

Many jurisdictions impose an additional requirement for the admission of confessions; these jurisdictions follow the corpus delicti rule and require corroboration. In these jurisdictions, apart from the defendant's confession, there must be independent evidence that a crime was committed. For example, in a robbery case, the store owner would have to testify that he found his locks broken and discovered money or merchandise missing. The corroboration need not show the identity of the perpetrator of the crime; it need show only that a crime was committed. The prosecutor ordinarily presents the corroborating evidence first and then calls the witness who will testify about the accused's confession to the crime.

[3] ADOPTIVE ADMISSIONS

[a] OVERVIEW

In personal admissions, the party-opponent himself or herself says or writes the statement constituting the admission. In adoptive admissions, a third party says or writes the statement. The party-opponent then manifests assent to the statement in some fashion. In the words of Federal Rule of Evidence 801(d)(2)(B), the party "manifested that [the party] adopted or believed [the assertion] to be true." When a criminal-accused signs a confession typed by a secretary at the police station, the accused is manifesting assent to the contents of the writing. A party-opponent can manifest assent expressly or impliedly, even by silence.

[b] EXPRESS ADOPTION

The foundation includes these elements:

1. A declarant made a statement.

2. The declarant made the statement in the party's presence.

3. The party heard and understood the statement. The declarant's statement is thus offered for a nonhearsay purpose—to show its effect on the state of mind of the party.

4. The party made a statement which expressed agreement with the declarant's statement. It is not enough that the party referred to or repeated the declarant's statement; the party must manifest agreement with the substantive content of the declarant's assertion.

Most jurisdictions treat these foundational facts as Rule 104(b) issues. Hence, for example, the proponent need present only sufficient evidence to create a permissive inference that the party-opponent heard the declarant's statement. The jury ultimately decides whether the party-opponent heard the statement.

To illustrate this doctrine, we shall use a tort action involving a hit-and-run accident. On July 1, 2017, the plaintiff, Ms. Waylen, was crossing a street in downtown Iowa City when a car struck her and fled the scene. The plaintiff's complaint alleges that the driver of the car was the defendant, Brad Benton. Benton works as a salesperson at an electronics store in Iowa City. The defendant denies any involvement in the accident. In his pretrial deposition, he claimed that he was on vacation in Mexico on the date of the accident. The plaintiff is the proponent. The plaintiff calls Mr. George Nickmeyer as her next witness. Mr. Nickmeyer testifies that he is the manager of the store where Benton works.

P   Mr. Nickmeyer, WHAT are your duties as manager?

W   I'm generally in charge of everything—purchasing, finance, personnel, you name it, and I do it at the store. It's a pretty small operation.

P   Please tell us more about your personnel responsibilities.

W   It's a big area with lots of responsibilities. I make sure that everyone is signed up for fringe benefits, medical plans, and the like. I also keep track of work days and vacations. We don't have an old-fashioned time clock.

P   HOW do you keep track of vacation days? (1)

W   I keep a personal log of when people work and when they're off. Then at the end of each month I prepare a summary for each employee and have them verify its accuracy.

P	HOW do you do that? (2), (3)
W	I hand them the statement. At the end of each month, everyone checks by my office to inspect their work and vacation statement. They read it, and then they sign it.
P	Your Honor, I request that this be marked plaintiff's exhibit number one for identification.
J	It will be so marked.
P	Please let the record reflect that I am showing the exhibit to the opposing counsel.
J	The record will so reflect.
P	Permission to approach the witness?
J	Granted.
P	Mr. Nickmeyer, I now hand you plaintiff's exhibit number one for identification. WHAT is it? (1), (4)
W	It's Brad Benton's statement for the month of July 2017.
P	HOW do you recognize it? (1)
W	I was the one who prepared it; I recognize the contents and the form. In addition, I see Brad's signature at the bottom. He's worked for me for over three years.
P	HOW many times have you seen the defendant sign his name? (4)
W	I can't give you a precise number, but I've probably seen him do it dozens of times during that period. Like I said, the employees come by at the end of every month to sign these statements right in my presence.
P	HOW was this form prepared? (2), (3), (4)
W	I always do it the same way. I don't want any hassles with them over their vacation time. I call them into the office or they stop by on their own, read the statement while I'm present, and then put their John Hancock on it.
P	Your Honor, I now offer plaintiff's exhibit number one for identification into evidence as plaintiff's exhibit number one.
O	Your Honor, I must object on the ground that this is inadmissible hearsay. There's obviously an inadequate foundation for a business entry.
P	Your Honor, may I be heard?
J	Yes.
P	I'm not offering this exhibit as a business entry. I'm offering it as an adoptive admission. Mr. Nickmeyer prepared the form, but his testimony shows that the defendant had an opportunity to read and check it before

signing it. By signing it, the defendant manifested his assent to the accuracy of the form. The form lists July 1, 2017, as a workday for the defendant—not a vacation day. (4)

J   Objection overruled. The exhibit will be received.

P   Mr. Nickmeyer, let me direct your attention to the extreme, left-hand margin of the exhibit. WHAT is listed on that margin?

W   That margin lists each day of the month.

P   Now let me direct your attention to the middle column of the form and the column on the extreme right-hand margin. WHAT do those columns represent?

W   The middle column is for checkmarks indicating workdays. The column on the right is for vacation days. If someone works a particular day, I place a checkmark in the middle of the form. If they're on vacation, I place the check in the right-hand column.

P   Please look at the columns for July 1st, 2017.

W   O.K.

P   WHERE is the checkmark for July 1st—in the middle or on the right-hand margin?

W   It's in the middle.

P   Again, WHAT does the middle column represent?

W   Workdays.

P   Your Honor, I now request permission to circulate the exhibit to the jurors for their inspection.

J   Certainly.

[c] IMPLIED ADOPTION BY SILENCE—"TACIT ADMISSION"

Sometimes, if a person stands silent in the face of an accusation, we may infer the person's assent to the accusation from his or her silence. Thus, there can be an implied adoption by silence; the courts sometimes refer to this doctrine as "tacit admission." The foundation includes these elements:

1.   The declarant made a statement.

2.   The statement was an accusation against the party-opponent.

3.   The declarant made the statement in the party's presence.

4.   The party heard and understood the statement.

5.   The party had the opportunity to deny the statement.

6.   The party either remained silent or made an evasive or equivocal reply.

7.   Under similar circumstances, a reasonable innocent person would have immediately denied the accusation. While the preceding six elements are foundational facts falling under Rule 104(b), this element presents a mixed

question of law and fact. For that reason, the judge resolves this element. (Of course, even if the judge admits the evidence under this doctrine, during their deliberations the jurors can decide not to draw that inference.)

Our fact situation is another tort case arising from a collision. The plaintiff, Mr. Girard, alleges that the defendant, Ms. Ratner, caused the accident by disregarding a stop sign. The investigating officer was Highway Patrolman Kuns. The plaintiff calls Patrolman Kuns. He has already identified himself and testified that he responded to the accident scene. The plaintiff is the proponent.

P	WHAT did you do when you responded to the scene?
W	I immediately sought out the two drivers.
P	WHO were the drivers?
W	Your client, Mr. Girard, and Ms. Ratner.
P	WHERE is Mr. Girard now?
W	At the table over there.
P	HOW is he dressed?
W	He's wearing a gray business suit and blue tie.
P	Your Honor, please let the record reflect that the witness has identified the plaintiff.
J	It will so reflect.
P	WHERE is Ms. Ratner now?
W	At the other table there.
P	HOW is she dressed?
W	She has on a pink dress and red shoes.
P	Your Honor, please let the record reflect that the witness has also identified the defendant.
J	It will so reflect.
P	WHERE did you find the plaintiff and defendant at the accident scene?
W	They were standing on the northeast corner of the intersection.
P	HOW close were they to each other?
W	Right next to each other.
P	WHAT were they doing?
W	They were talking.
P	WHAT were they talking about?
W	The accident.
P	WHAT, if anything, did Mr. Girard tell the defendant about the accident? (1), (2)

O	Your Honor, I object to that question on the ground that it calls for hearsay.
P	Your Honor, may we approach the bench?
J	Yes.
P	I offer to prove that Mr. Girard told the defendant she had run a stop sign and that she adopted the statement by remaining silent. I am using Mr. Girard's statement for a nonhearsay purpose; I am not offering the statement itself for its truth. I simply want to prove that the plaintiff made the statement and the defendant then adopted it.
O	There's been no foundation for an adoptive admission yet.
J	I will admit the statement subject to a motion to strike.
P	Officer Kuns, let me repeat the question. WHAT, if anything, did Mr. Girard tell the defendant about the accident? (1), (2)
W	He told her that she had caused the accident by running a stop sign. He said she was as blind as a bat.
P	WHAT language was Mr. Girard speaking in? (4)
W	English.
P	HOW close was Mr. Girard to the defendant when he made that statement? (3)
W	Two feet away at most. As I said, they were standing talking.
P	HOW much noise was there when Mr. Girard made the statement? (4), (5)
W	It was pretty quiet. The traffic congestion had died down.
P	HOW many other people were talking to the defendant at the time? (4), (5)
W	No one else.
P	WHOM was Mr. Girard facing when he made the statement? (4), (5)
W	He was looking right at Ms. Ratner.
P	HOW was she facing? (4), (5)
W	She was facing him.
P	WHAT was Mr. Girard's tone of voice when he made the statement? (5), (7)
W	He was obviously excited, but he wasn't screaming at her.
P	WHAT threats, if any, did Mr. Girard make against the defendant at the time? (5), (7)
W	None. He was upset, but he wasn't menacing or anything like that.
P	WHAT gestures did Mr. Girard make? (5), (7)

W	He was animated, but he wasn't making a fist or pointing a finger in Ms. Ratner's face. He was just exasperated.
P	WHAT was the defendant's facial expression immediately after Mr. Girard made the statement? (7)
W	She looked worried.
P	WHERE did she look? (4), (5), (7)
W	Right after he made the statement, she looked down and away from the plaintiff.
P	WHAT, if anything, did the defendant say then? (6)
W	Nothing.
P	WHAT was her response to Mr. Girard's statement that she had run the stop sign? (6)
W	None. She didn't say anything in response to his remark.

[4] VICARIOUS ADMISSIONS

[a] IN CIVIL CASES

In vicarious admissions, the basis for imputing the statement to the party-opponent is the party's close relationship with the declarant. A principal debtor's statement may be admitted against a surety, the statements of a predecessor in title against the present titleholder, and the statements of an agent against the principal. The foundation consists of demonstrating the relation between the declarant and the party-opponent. Once the relation has been demonstrated, the declarant's statements are vicariously admissible against the party-opponent. There is currently a division of authority over the question of whether vicarious admissions must be based on the declarant's personal knowledge.

Most vicarious admissions in civil cases are statements made by agents and admitted against the agent's principal. The traditional view is that the declarant must have been an authorized spokesperson for the principal. Under this view, it is not sufficient that the declarant was an agent or employee of the party-opponent. The declarant must have been a special type of agent, namely, a spokesperson authorized to make statements on the principal's behalf. In the words of Federal Rule of Evidence 801(d)(2)(C), "the statement" was made "by a person whom the party authorized to make a statement on the subject." In these jurisdictions, the foundation includes the following elements:

1. The declarant was an agent of the party-opponent.

2. The party-opponent authorized the declarant to make the particular statements. In *Bourjaily v. United States*, 483 U.S. 171, 107 S. Ct. 2775, 97 L. Ed. 2d 144 (1987), the Court held that Rule 104(a) governs the foundational facts for the coconspirator exemption codified in Rule 801(d)(2)(E). Rule 801(d)(2) was amended effective December 1, 1997, by adding a sentence at the end of the subdivision. The accompanying Advisory Committee Note explained that the purpose of the amendment was to extend the same treatment to the "preliminary questions relating to the declarant's authority under subdivision (C)."

3. The statement is inconsistent with a position the party-opponent is taking at trial. More precisely, the statement must be logically relevant to an issue the proponent has a right to prove at trial.

The fact situation is a suit against an insurance company. Delta Corporation sues Grant Insurance Company. The complaint alleges that the defendant insured the plaintiff against fire; a fire occurred on the plaintiff's premises and caused $200,000 in damages; and the defendant has wrongfully refused to compensate the plaintiff. The policy excluded any fire that the plaintiff's employees negligently started. In discovery, the defendant obtained a copy of a report the plaintiff's safety investigator, Mr. Grant Richards, prepared. The report includes the finding that one contributing cause of the fire was some careless welding by plaintiff's employees; the welder negligently cut into a furnace and permitted flames to escape. During its case-in-chief, the defendant calls Mr. Richards. In many jurisdictions, the defendant could treat him as an adverse witness under Rule 611(c)(2) and conduct the direct examination as cross-examination and use leading questions. For our purposes, we shall restrict the defense attorney to non-leading questions. The defendant is the proponent. Mr. Richards has already identified himself.

P	WHERE do you work? (1)
W	I work for Delta Corporation in Albuquerque.
P	HOW long have you worked for them? (1)
W	Seven years, give or take a few months.
P	WHAT is your job with Delta Corporation? (2)
W	I am the chief safety and accident investigator.
P	HOW long have you held that position? (2)
W	The last five years.
P	WHERE were you on November 13, 2017? (2)
W	At our plant in Santa Fe.
P	WHAT were you doing there? (2)
W	I was investigating the fire that had occurred the day before.
P	HOW long did you spend investigating the fire? (2)
W	The whole day.
P	WHAT did you do when you finished the investigation? (2)
W	As is my normal practice, I prepared a report of the investigation.
P	Your Honor, I request that this be marked defense exhibit F for identification.
J	It will be so marked.
P	Please let the record reflect that I am showing the exhibit to the opposing counsel.

J	It will so reflect.
P	I request permission to approach the witness.
J	Permission granted.
P	Mr. Richards, I now hand you defense exhibit F for identification. WHAT is it? (2)
W	It's my report on the fire.
P	HOW can you recognize it? (2)
W	I recognize my handwriting on the last page. I also generally recall the report's contents.
P	Again, WHAT are your duties for Delta Corporation? (2)
W	As I said before, I'm the safety and accident investigator.
P	In general terms, WHAT is the subject of this particular report?
W	It relates to the fire I investigated as part of my duties.
P	WHY did you prepare this particular report? (2)
W	It's part of my job. In fact, the vice-president for operations ordered me to get that report finished and submitted as soon as possible.
P	Your Honor, I now offer defense exhibit F for identification into evidence as defense exhibit F.
J	It will be received.
P	Mr. Richards, please turn to page 18 of exhibit F and read finding #4 to the jury. (3)
W	The report reads, "Another contributing factor may have been our own employees' carelessness. Some of our welders were evidently working next to furnace #3 on the second floor. Some eyewitness reports indicated that the welders accidentally cut into the furnace, releasing the flames that started the fire."

A few jurisdictions limit this doctrine to statements made to third parties outside the business organization. In this hypothetical, the document was an internal report; Richards submitted the report to his superiors in the corporation. Those jurisdictions would exclude the report. Even in those jurisdictions, the report would be admissible if Richards prepared the report for a third party outsider such as a government safety agency. The trend is to abandon this limitation. Federal Rule of Evidence 801(d)(2)(C) follows the trend and would permit the admission of Richards' report as a vicarious admission.

The emerging view is that the party-opponent need not have authorized the particular statement; the declarant does not have to have been a spokesperson. Under the emerging view, it is sufficient that the declarant was an agent of the party-opponent and the statement related to the agent's employment duties. Federal Rule of Evidence 801(d)(2)(D) opts for this view. That Rule authorizes the admission of "a statement . . .

made by the party's agent or employee on a matter within the scope of that relationship and while it existed." Under this view, the only foundational elements are:

1. The declarant was an agent of the party-opponent.

2. The declarant made the statement while he or she was an agent.

3. The statement related to the agent's employment duties. The proponent first elicits testimony about the agent's employment duties. The proponent then asks the agent "about" a topic related to the duties. As previously stated, *Bourjaily v. United States*, 483 U.S. 171, 107 S. Ct. 2775, 97 L. Ed. 2d 144 (1987) announces that Rule 104(a) governs the foundational facts for the coconspirator exemption codified in subdivision 801(d)(2)(E). According to the accompanying Advisory Committee Note, the December 1, 1997 amendment to Rule 801(d)(2) was intended to extend the same treatment to "preliminary questions relating to . . . the agency or employment relationship and scope thereof under subdivision (D)."

4. The statement is inconsistent with a position the party-opponent is taking at trial; the statement is logically relevant to an issue the proponent has a right to prove at trial.

Our fact situation is a tort action arising from a collision. Ms. Henning, the plaintiff, alleges that Carrington Company's driver, Mr. Julius, negligently caused the accident. The only named defendant is the company, Carrington. During the plaintiff's case-in-chief, she calls Mr. Julius as a witness. As in the previous hypothetical, many courts would permit the proponent to treat the witness as an adverse witness and conduct the direct examination with leading questions as if it were cross-examination. However, for teaching purposes, our proponent will use non-leading questions. Mr. Julius has already identified himself.

P	WHERE do you work? (1)
W	I work for the Carrington warehouse here in Billings.
P	HOW long have you worked there? (1)
W	Eight years.
P	WHAT are your duties? (1)
W	I'm a driver. I haul our deliveries all over the United States. I do mostly intrastate moves, but I occasionally do cross-country moves.
P	Mr. Julius, WHERE were you on the afternoon of October 13, 2017? (2)
W	I was driving along Highway 84 headed for Colorado.
P	WHO were you working for that day? (2)
W	My regular employer, Carrington.
P	WHAT happened that afternoon? (2)
W	I was involved in an accident with a Ms. Henning. (*Here the proponent would elicit facts about the collision itself.*)
P	WHAT happened immediately after the accident? (3)

W	I talked to the police officer who investigated the accident.
P	WHAT was his name? (3)
W	I think his name was Patrolman Blue.
P	WHAT, if anything, did you tell him about your speed just before the collision? (3), (4)
O	Your Honor, I object to that question on the ground that it calls for hearsay.
P	Your Honor, may we approach the bench?
J	Yes.
P	Your Honor, I offer to prove that the witness will admit he said he was going 70 miles an hour. My theory of admissibility is that Mr. Julius' statement about his speed is a vicarious admission against his employer.
O	Carrington hires drivers to drive rather than to act as spokespersons.
P	As you know, Your Honor, this jurisdiction recently adopted the Federal Rules of Evidence. Rule 801 authorizes the admission of agents' statements so long as they relate to the agent's employment duties. This statement relates to the speed at which Mr. Julius was driving.
J	The objection will be overruled.
P	Mr. Julius, let me repeat the question. WHAT, if anything, did you tell Patrolman Blue about your speed just before the collision? (3), (4)
W	I told him I thought I was going about 70 miles an hour. I was a little behind schedule, and I was trying to make up time.
P	WHAT is the posted speed limit on the stretch of highway where the collision occurred?
W	55 miles an hour.

[b] IN CRIMINAL CASES

The criminal counterpart of the exception for agents' statements is the co-conspirator doctrine. Federal Rule of Evidence 801(d)(2)(E) states the doctrine. That Rule exempts a "statement . . . made by the party's coconspirator during and in furtherance of the conspiracy." The foundation includes these elements:

1. There was a conspiracy.

2. The conspiracy was in progress when the declarant made the statement. The conspiracy continues at least until the conspirators attempt to commit the crime. If the crime is a theft offense, the conspiracy also continues until the conspirators divide the proceeds of the theft. However, in most jurisdictions, absent an express agreement, the conspiracy does not continue while the individual conspirators later try to evade arrest and prosecution.

3. The declarant was a co-conspirator.

4. The declarant made the statement in furtherance of the conspiracy. For

instance, the declarant furthers the conspiracy by attempting to recruit new conspirators or updating current conspirators on the state of their plans. If the declarant has already been arrested, his or her confession is usually not deemed to promote the conspiracy.

5. The accused was a member of the conspiracy. The accused need not be a member of the conspiracy when the declarant makes the statement; if the accused later joins the conspiracy, the accused is deemed to ratify the earlier statements.

In *Bourjaily v. United States*, 483 U.S. 171, 107 S. Ct. 2775, 97 L. Ed. 2d 144 (1987), the Supreme Court announced that in deciding whether the prosecution has established all the foundational elements, under Rule 104(a) the trial judge may consider the content of the proffered statement itself. After *Bourjaily*, the uniform view among the lower federal courts was that although the prosecution may use the content of the proffered statement to help establish the foundation, standing alone the statement itself is insufficient to lay the foundation. The December 1, 1997 amendment to Rule 801 codified that view.

To lay the foundation, the prosecutor often calls an informer or a conspirator who has turned state's evidence. Our fact situation is a prosecution for conspiracy to sell cocaine. The accused is Mr. George Sherr. The indictment alleges that the accused conspired with Mr. James Blanton. The prosecution calls Mr. Donald Peterson as a witness. The prosecutor hopes to use Mr. Peterson's testimony to prove the intent to sell. The witness has already identified himself. The prosecution is the proponent.

P   WHAT is your occupation?

W   I am a police officer, a member of the Tucson Police Department.

P   WHAT are your duties?

W   I specialize in undercover work for the Narcotics Division.

P   HOW long have you done that type of work?

W   For the last three years.

P   WHERE were you on the evening of September 3, 2016? (1)

W   I was at James Blanton's house near the City Hall in Tucson.

P   WHO else was there? (1), (3), (5)

W   It was just me, Blanton, and the accused.

P   WHAT happened while you were there? (1)

W   Blanton showed me some bags containing a drug. Both Blanton and the accused referred to it as cocaine.

P   WHAT happened after Blanton showed you the bags? (1)

W   I pretended to get high on some marijuana; and while I was doing that, Blanton and the defendant discussed their plans for getting more cocaine.

P   WHAT plans did they discuss? (1)

W	Blanton said he had a contact in Mexico for good cocaine; and the accused said he could fly down in a small plane, pick up the cocaine, and smuggle it back across the border.
P	WHEN did they say they would carry out these plans? (2)
W	Over the next couple of months.
P	WHAT happened after they discussed their plans?
W	The accused took me home.
P	WHAT happened the next day? (2)
W	I met Blanton for lunch.
P	WHAT happened during the lunch? (4)
W	Blanton invited me to help the accused and him carry out their plans.
P	HOW did he want you to help him? (4)
W	He said he wanted me to hide some bags of cocaine in my apartment. He said he thought it would be a good idea to divide up his cache rather than storing it in only one place.
P	HOW did you respond? (4)
W	I said that I wanted to make certain there was something in it for me.
P	WHAT, if anything, did Blanton say then? (4)
O	Your Honor, I object to that question on the ground that it calls for hearsay.
P	Your Honor, may we approach the bench?
J	Yes.
P	Your Honor, I offer to prove that the witness will testify that Blanton said he and the accused were going to sell the cocaine and make enough money to pay the witness $10,000. The testimony is directly relevant to prove the intent to sell. Since Blanton was the accused's co-conspirator, Blanton's statement is vicariously admissible against the accused.
J	The objection will be overruled.
P	Mr. Peterson, let me repeat the question. WHAT did Mr. Blanton say when you said you wanted to make certain there was something in the proposal for you? (4)
W	He said that he and the accused weren't simply stockpiling the cocaine supply for their personal use. He told me that they intended to sell the cocaine. He was certain that they would make enough money to pay me $10,000 for the use of my apartment.

PART D.   Hearsay Exceptions Based Primarily on a Showing of Reliability

§ 10.04   IN GENERAL

As we saw in the last section, a proponent offering a statement as the admission of a party-opponent need not establish the reliability of the statement or any necessity to resort to the statement. In contrast, many hearsay exceptions require a showing of reliability. These exceptions fall into two categories. In one category, the exception is usually a spinoff of the old *res gestae* doctrine; and there is an inference of sincerity on the part of the declaration. Sections 10.08 through 10.11 of this chapter focus on the exceptions falling into this category. The second category includes primarily documentary statements. There is something about the process of generating these types of writings which creates an inference of the reliability of the written statement. Sections 10.05 through 10.07 of this chapter discuss those hearsay exceptions.

§ 10.05   BUSINESS ENTRIES

[1]   THE DOCTRINE

At common law, business entries are exceptionally admissible. Federal Rule of Evidence 803(6) restates the modern doctrine:

> The following [is] not excluded by the rule against hearsay . . .: A record of an act, event, condition, opinion, or diagnosis if:
>
> (A)   the record was made at or near the time by—or from information transmitted by—someone with knowledge;
>
> (B)   the record was kept in the course of a regularly conducted activity of a business, organization, occupation, or calling, whether or not for profit;
>
> (C)   making the record was a regular practice of that activity;
>
> (D)   all these conditions are shown by the testimony of the custodian or another qualified person, or by a certification that complies with Rule 902(11) or (12) or with a statute permitting certification; and
>
> (E)   the opponent does not show that the source of information or the method or circumstances of preparation indicate a lack of trustworthiness.

In the case of business entries, the circumstantial guarantee of trustworthiness is that since the entry is routine, the business' employees have developed habits of precision in gathering and reporting the data. The employees' habits help to ensure the reliability of the report. There is also necessity for resorting to the hearsay report. If a business conducts hundreds or thousands of similar transactions during a year, it is doubtful whether any employee will remember the particular transaction recorded in the entry. Even when an employee remembers, the employee's memory is likely to be incomplete or hazy. Thus, the business entry is probably the most reliable evidence available.

[2]   ELEMENTS OF THE FOUNDATION

Some commentators have suggested that the Federal Rules of Evidence "collapse" the traditional, common-law elements of the business entry foundation into a single requirement for a general showing of reliability. However, most commentators and courts still assume that the proponent must establish the following foundational elements:

1. The report was prepared by a person with a business relationship with the company. It is ideal if the person is an employee of the company. However, the person might also work for a parent, subsidiary, or affiliated company.

2. The informant (the ultimate source of the report) had a business duty to report the information. This requirement is traceable to the leading case of *Johnson v. Lutz*, 253 N.Y. 124, 170 N.E. 517 (1930). There the court held that a report is not prepared in the course of business unless all the persons contributing to the report have a business duty to do so. In that case, the business entity was the police department. The parts of the police report reflecting bystanders' statements did not qualify as business entries, since the civilian bystanders were not employees of the police department.[1] The informant's business duty is one of the guarantees of the report's trustworthiness. The test is the existence of the business duty, not the informant's status as an employee of the business. Thus, the employee of a subsidiary corporation would qualify, since he or she would have a business duty to the parent entity. The Advisory Committee Note to Rule 803(6) approvingly refers to *Johnson*. (Some courts apply the business entry exception to hotel registration records when the foundation includes proof that the hotel routinely demands proof of identity before allowing someone to register as a guest.)

3. The informant had personal knowledge of the facts or events reported.

4. The written report was prepared contemporaneously with the facts or events.

5. It was a routine practice of the business to prepare such reports.

6. The report was reduced to written form.

7. The report was made in the regular course of business. The expression, "regular course of business," at least requires that the entry be related to the nature of the business. For instance, a sales slip is obviously related to the nature of a retail merchandise business. *Palmer v. Hoffman*, 318 U.S. 109, 64 S. Ct. 477, 87 L. Ed. 645 (1943) adds another level of meaning to "regular course of business." The lower courts and commentators have construed *Palmer* as meaning that reports specially prepared for litigation are not made "in the regular course of business." If the trial judge finds that the business entry is in reality a special litigation report, the judge has discretion to exclude the entry as being suspect and unreliable. The Advisory Committee Note to Rule 803(6) also approvingly cites *Palmer*.

---

[1] The passage represents double hearsay under Rule 805: The author of the report asserts that the bystander made an assertion. Since the bystander has no business duty, the proponent cannot apply Rule 803(6) to both levels of hearsay. However, suppose that the bystander's statement qualified as an excited utterance. The proponent could then tack Rule 803(6) together with Rule 803(2).

8. The entry is factual in nature. Rule 803(6) relaxes this requirement by expressly allowing the admission of an "opinion . . . or diagnosis." However, some courts do not apply this language literally. For instance, these courts balk at admitting highly evaluative opinions such as psychiatric diagnoses. The standards for some psychiatric diagnoses are "soft" and subjective, and there is an acute need to cross-examine the expert who arrived at the diagnosis.

The witness need not have personal knowledge of the entry's preparation. In fact, the witness rarely has such knowledge. The witness is ordinarily the business' records custodian or librarian. Rule 803(6)(D) permits foundational testimony by "the custodian or another qualified witness." The witness testifies to his or her connection with the business and then describes the habitual method with which the business prepares and maintains its reports. The proponent lays the foundation for such habit by following the procedure outlined in § 6.03 of Chapter 6. The habit evidence has sufficient probative value to support a finding that the business followed that procedure on the occasion in question.

[3] SAMPLE FOUNDATION

The fact situation is a contract suit. The plaintiff is Armor Corporation. Its complaint alleges that it delivered 500 stereophonic speakers to Hyatt Corporation and that the defendant wrongfully failed to pay for the speakers. The defendant filed an answer, generally denying the complaint's allegations. The plaintiff wants to introduce a Delivery Sheet, stating that its employees delivered the 500 speakers to the defendant. The plaintiff calls Mr. James Merton as a witness. Mr. Merton has already identified himself. The plaintiff is the proponent.

P   WHERE do you work?

W   I am the records librarian for Armor Corporation.

P   HOW long have you held that position?

W   About six years.

P   WHAT are your duties as records librarian?

W   I establish company-wide procedures for preparing records. I ensure that the records that are prepared are properly filed, and I'm finally in charge of records retirement and destruction.

P   Your Honor, I request that this be marked plaintiff's exhibit number three for identification.

J   It will be so marked.

P   Please let the record reflect that I am showing the exhibit to the opposing counsel.

J   It will so reflect.

P   I request permission to approach the witness.

J   Permission granted.

P	Mr. Merton, I now hand you plaintiff's exhibit number three for identification. WHAT is it?

Authentication

The complete foundation would include proof of the document's authenticity. See §§ 4.02 and 4.03 of Chapter 4.

Best Evidence

The complete foundation will also include proof of compliance with the best evidence rule. See Chapter 8.

Hearsay

P	WHO prepared this document? (1)
W	Well, it seems to have been prepared by Bob Grant.
P	HOW do you know that? (1)
W	I recognize his handwriting style. I've seen his writing on hundreds of occasions.
P	WHO is Bob Grant? (1)
W	He's one of our delivery personnel.
P	As a delivery man, WHAT are Mr. Grant's duties? (2)
W	He picks up merchandise in our warehouse in Scranton, makes sure that it gets to the customer, and prepares the paperwork on the delivery.
P	WHICH of your employees are authorized to prepare the paperwork? (3)
W	Only the delivery person in charge of that particular delivery. That's the employee who fills out the delivery report or sheet.
P	WHEN does the delivery person make out the report? (4)
W	He's supposed to make it out as soon as they make the delivery. At the very latest, they make it out when they get back to our office.
P	HOW often do your employees prepare these reports? (5)
W	Every time they make a delivery. I'd say that they send us 50 to 80 of those delivery sheets each week.
P	WHAT form does the report take? (6)
W	It's a standard, written report we call a Delivery Sheet. Like the one we have here, exhibit number three or whatever the number is.
P	WHY do you require that the delivery personnel prepare these reports? (7)
W	There are all sorts of business reasons for the reports—accounting, inventory, taxes. You just can't run an efficient, profitable business establishment unless you keep very, very close tabs on your deliveries.
P	WHAT does the delivery person do with the report after he prepares it?
W	He hands it to someone in our office.

P	WHAT does your office do with it?
W	We store it in a separate file, including all the Delivery Sheets for that week.
P	WHERE did you find plaintiff's exhibit number three for identification?
W	In the file for that week's Delivery Sheets.
P	WHEN did you remove it from that file?
W	Just this morning before trial.
P	Your Honor, I now offer plaintiff's exhibit number three for identification into evidence as plaintiff's exhibit number three.
O	Your Honor, I object to the exhibit's introduction on the ground that the exhibit is incompetent hearsay.
J	The objection will be overruled, and the exhibit will be received.
P	Mr. Merton, please read the circled part of the exhibit to the jury.
W	That part reads, "January 18—delivered 500 stereo speakers to Hyatt Corp."
P	Your Honor, I request permission to submit the exhibit to the jurors for their personal inspection.
J	Permission granted.

In 2000, Rule 902 was amended to provide that a proper attesting certificate renders a business record self-authenticating. Construed together, Rules 803(6) and 902(11) permit the proponent to dispense with live, sponsoring testimony.

§ 10.06 OFFICIAL RECORDS

[1] THE DOCTRINE

The second major documentary exception to the hearsay rule is the official records doctrine. Just as business employees presumably are careful in gathering and recording information for their employers, public employees presumably are diligent in gathering and recording information for their employer, the government. For this reason, the common law and the Federal Rules admit official records as well as business entries. Federal Rule of Evidence 803(8) states the basic doctrine:

> The following [is] not excluded by the rule against hearsay . . .: A record or statement of a public office if:
>
> (A)   it sets out:
>
>   (i)   the office's activities;
>
>   (ii)   a matter observed while under a legal duty to report, but not including, in a criminal case, a matter observed by law-enforcement personnel; or
>
>   (iii)   in a civil case or against the government in a criminal case, factual findings from a legally authorized investigation; and

(B)   the opponent does not show that the source of information or other circumstances indicate a lack of trustworthiness.

Section 4.04 of Chapter 4 discusses the authentication of official records. As that section noted, the proponent of an official record rarely presents live, sponsoring testimony to authenticate the record. In most instances, live testimony is similarly unnecessary to lay the foundation for the official records exception to the hearsay rule. Two doctrines make the live testimony unnecessary. The first doctrine is judicial notice. The judge will ordinarily judicially notice the statute, regulation, or custom requiring that the public official prepare the record. Next, if the attested copy is fair on its face (complete with no erasures), the document's face creates a permissive inference that the officials followed the proper procedures in preparing the particular record.

[2] ELEMENTS OF THE FOUNDATION

At common law, a complete foundation for the official records hearsay exception includes these elements:

1. The record was prepared at or near the time of the fact or event recorded. Some cases and statutes no longer explicitly require this element. Federal Rule of Evidence 803(8) is illustrative; its language does not impose this requirement. In jurisdictions dispensing with this element, the only requirement is that the entry be properly prepared. If, long after the original event, the official discovers an error in the record and follows prescribed procedures for making a corrected entry, the corrected entry will qualify as an official record.

2. The record is in official custody.

3. The record is open to public inspection. The early, English cases impose this requirement. Many jurisdictions have dispensed with this element; in these jurisdictions, it is sufficient that the record is in official custody. Rule 803(8) adopts the latter view.

4. The record was properly prepared. The official must substantially comply with the procedures prescribed for the report's preparation.

5. The preparer was a public official.

6. The official had a duty to record the fact.

7. The official had personal knowledge of the fact. Rule 803(8)(A)(iii) relaxes this requirement "in a civil case or against the government in a criminal case." That subsection allows the admission of "factual findings from a legally authorized investigation." Some lower courts construed this language as permitting the admission of findings about events even when the investigating officer lacked firsthand knowledge of the event. The Supreme Court adopted that construction in *Beech Aircraft Corp. v. Rainey*, 488 U.S. 153, 109 S. Ct. 439, 102 L. Ed. 2d 445 (1988).

8. The entry is factual in nature. In footnote 13 in *Beech Aircraft*, the Court stated that it was "express[ing] no opinion as to whether legal conclusions contained in an official report are admissible as 'findings of fact' under Rule 803(8)(C)."

Most lower courts have ruled that legal conclusions are inadmissible.

[3]   SAMPLE FOUNDATIONS

We shall first illustrate the admission of an official record without live testimony. The fact situation is a quiet title action. The plaintiff, Mr. Thelan, and the defendant, Mr. Garrett, both claim title to the same parcel of land in Miami, Florida. Both claim from the same grantor, but Mr. Thelan contends that he recorded his deed first. Mr. Thelan proposes to offer a properly attested copy of the recordation of the deed in the County Clerk's office. The copy shows the date of recording. The plaintiff is the proponent.

P   Your Honor, I request that this be marked plaintiff's exhibit number four for identification.

J   It will be so marked.

P   Please let the record reflect that I am showing the exhibit to the opposing counsel.

J   It will so reflect.

P   I now offer plaintiff's exhibit number four for identification into evidence as plaintiff's exhibit number four.

O   Your Honor, I object to the introduction of the exhibit on the ground that the exhibit is hearsay.

P   Your Honor, may we approach the bench?

J   Yes.

O   Your Honor, this record is an assertive out-of-court statement, and the plaintiff is obviously going to use it for its truth, namely, the date of the recordation of his deed. The exhibit is undeniably hearsay.

P   That's true, but the record falls within the official record exception to the hearsay rule.

O   There's been no foundation for that exception. No sponsoring witness has come forward to lay the foundation.

P   Live testimony is unnecessary. Your Honor, you can judicially notice Civil Code section 1477 which requires the County Clerk to record deeds relating to land in the county. Moreover, the attached copy is fair on its face; it's complete, and there are no erasures or unexplained marks. The face of the document creates an inference that the public official properly carried out his duties. The attesting certificate renders this exhibit self-authenticating under Rule 902(4).

J   I agree. The objection will be overruled, and the exhibit will be received.

P   Your Honor, I request permission to read the exhibit to the jury.

J   Permission granted.

P   Ladies and gentlemen, I am about to read this exhibit to you. The exhibit purports to be a Xerox copy of a page from the records of the Dade

County Clerk. The exhibit reads, "Date of recordation—January 13, 2016, grantor—Paul A. Peterson, grantee—John D. Thelan, parcel number—17,886." Your Honor, I now request permission to hand the exhibit to the jurors for their inspection.

J   Permission granted.

In the next hypothetical, we shall use live testimony. The plaintiff, Mr. Schmitt, has sued the defendant, the State of Missouri. Mr. Schmitt sustained personal injuries when his car left a Missouri highway and crashed. Mr. Schmitt alleges that the degree of slope in the curve where he lost control of his car was too sharp. His expert will testify that for that type of road, any slope greater than 17 degrees would represent negligent design and engineering. Mr. Schmitt wants to introduce a Missouri Department of Transportation report, listing the degree of slope on the curve as 19 degrees. Mr. Schmitt calls Mr. Justin as a witness. Mr. Justin has already identified himself. The plaintiff is the proponent.

P   WHAT is your educational background?

W   I have bachelor's and master's degrees in civil engineering from the University of Missouri.

P   WHERE do you work? (5)

W   I am a civil engineer for the Missouri Department of Transportation.

P   WHAT is the Department of Transportation? (5)

W   It's an official department of our state government.

P   HOW long have you worked there? (5)

W   The past seven years.

P   Your Honor, I request that this be marked plaintiff's exhibit number six for identification.

J   It will be so marked.

P   Please let the record reflect that I am showing the exhibit to the opposing counsel.

J   It will so reflect.

P   I request permission to approach the witness.

J   Permission granted.

P   Mr. Justin, I now hand you plaintiff's exhibit number six for identification. WHAT is it?

W   It's a report I prepared on the curve on Missouri Highway 10 seven-tenths of a mile south of the Columbia turnoff.

P   WHERE have you been this morning?

W   Right here in the courtroom.

P   WHAT stretch of road have the witnesses this morning been talking about?

W	The same curve I surveyed in this report.
	WHEN did you make this survey? (1)
W	In early 2017.
P	WHY did you make the survey? (6)
W	The regional office decided to conduct a safety inspection of the area, and the local supervisor ordered me to do the field work.
P	WHO actually inspected the curve? (7)
W	I did personally.
P	WHO actually prepared the report? (7)
W	I did. Well, to be exact, I dictated it. A secretary typed it, and then I reviewed and signed it.
P	HOW long after the survey did you prepare the report? (1)
W	The very next day. I always follow that practice with surveys.
P	WHAT procedures are you supposed to follow in conducting this type of survey and preparing the report? (4)
W	The practice is that you both drive the road and walk it with appropriate surveying equipment. You take detailed notes and then have them immediately transcribed.
P	WHAT procedure did you actually follow? (4)
W	I did it by the book. As far as I know, I complied with all the required steps.
P	WHERE is this report ordinarily kept? (2)
W	In my office files at the Department's local office.
P	WHO can inspect the report? (3)
W	It's generally open to the public.
P	Your Honor, I now offer plaintiff's exhibit number six for identification into evidence as plaintiff's exhibit number six.
O	Your Honor, I object to the introduction of the exhibit on the ground that the exhibit is hearsay.
P	Your Honor, may we approach the bench?
J	Yes.
P	Your Honor, I concede that the exhibit is hearsay, but I submit that I've laid a complete foundation for the official record exception to the hearsay rule.
O	In general, that's true. However, an additional requirement is that the entry offered be factual. Page 10 of the report has a lot of conclusory

	opinions. I want to know whether the plaintiff's counsel intends to read that page to the jury.
J	(*To the proponent*) What is your intention?
P	I only want the witness to read one of the measurements listed on page seven.
O	Very well, I have no objection to that.
J	Then the exhibit will be received, and you have permission to have the witness read that portion of page seven to the jury. I won't let the exhibit itself go to the jury because it contains inadmissible opinion.
P	Mr. Justin, please read the first measurement on page seven to the jurors.
W	The report reads, "While at the scene, I measured the slope of the curve. I determined the angle to be 19 degrees."

§ 10.07   PAST RECOLLECTION RECORDED AND PRESENT RECOLLECTION REFRESHED OR REVIVED

[1]   PAST RECOLLECTION RECORDED

The next documentary hearsay exception is the past recollection recorded doctrine. Suppose that the witness on the stand cannot recall a particular fact or event. The witness's inability to recall supplies necessity for resorting to hearsay evidence. If at the time of the event, the witness had made a record of the fact or event, the record would be a reliable substitute for the witness's present recall. The recognition of this necessity and reliability led to the development of the past recollection recorded doctrine.

Federal Rule of Evidence 803(5) states the doctrine succinctly:

The following [is] not excluded by the rule against hearsay . . .: A record that:

(A)   is on a matter the witness once knew about but now cannot recall well enough to testify fully and accurately;

(B)   was made or adopted by the witness when the matter was fresh in the witness's memory; and

(C)   accurately reflects the witness's knowledge.

If the proponent can show that the exhibit satisfies the doctrine, the real evidence is the document. In many jurisdictions, since the real evidence is the document, the judge formally admits the document and permits it to be submitted to the jury. Other courts take a different position. They reason that the document is the functional equivalent of oral testimony and that it would place undue emphasis on that evidence to permit the jury to examine the document. This reasoning partially persuaded the drafters of the Federal Rules of Evidence. Federal Rule of Evidence 803(5) provides that "[i]f admitted, the record may be read into evidence but may be received as an exhibit only if offered by an adverse party." "Admitted" authorizes formal admission by the judge while the reference to "received" prohibits physical receipt of the exhibit by the jury.

The foundation for this hearsay exception includes these elements:

1.   The witness formerly gained personal knowledge of the fact or event recorded.

There is authority that if the declarant disavows personal knowledge, the proponent may rely on other testimony to establish this element of the foundation. *State v. Nava*, 177 Wn. App. 272, 311 P.3d 83 (2013).

2. The witness subsequently prepared a record of the facts. All courts accept the foundation if the witness personally prepared the record. *Most* courts accept the record if a third party prepared it but the witness verified it while the events were still fresh in the witness's memory. Some courts also accept cooperative past recollection recorded; witness #1 gives an accurate oral report to witness #2, and witness #2 testifies that he or she accurately transcribed the oral report. The cooperative theory necessitates that both witnesses appear at trial and testify. (Most jurisdictions now recognize the present sense impression exception codified in Federal Rule 803(1). If the judge is willing to apply that exception to witness #1's statement, witness #2's live testimony should suffice to justify the admission of the record.)

3. The witness prepared the record while the events were still fresh in his or her memory. The courts have interpreted Rule 803(5) as liberalizing this timing requirement. In *United States v. Patterson*, 678 F.2d 774 (9th Cir. 1982), the court found a declarant's memory sufficiently fresh despite a 10-month time lapse. *See also United States v. Senak*, 527 F.2d 129 (7th Cir. 1975), *cert. denied*, 425 U.S. 907 (1976) (a three-year delay).

4. The witness vouches that when he or she prepared the record, the record was accurate. Ideally, the witness will recall the very occasion on which he or she prepared the document. Alternatively, the witness may testify that he or she habitually records that type of information and that their habit is to record the information carefully. A police officer assigned to the traffic detail could give that type of testimony about measurements at accident scenes. Finally, in some jurisdictions, it is acceptable if the witness at least recognizes his or her handwriting on the document. In this last situation, in reality the witness is vouching for his or her own honesty; they are really testifying that they are an honest person and would not knowingly record false data.

5. At trial, the witness cannot completely and accurately recall the facts even after reviewing the document. The early view was that the witness had to completely forget the event. In other words, the witness had to "draw a complete blank." Most modern courts are of the view that it is sufficient if the witness's memory is partial or hazy. In the words of Federal Rule of Evidence 803(5), the witness cannot remember "fully and accurately."

As previously stated, on the one hand, Rule 803(5) can be interpreted as permitting the formal admission of the exhibit. On the other hand, the Rule forbids physically submitting the exhibit to the jurors for their inspection. *Maggipinto v. Reichman*, 607 F.2d 621 (3d Cir. 1979) (construing similar language in Rule 803(18)).

Our fact situation is a bank robbery prosecution. The government charges that Mr. Gary Vincent robbed the First National Bank in downtown Phoenix. The witness is Ms. Jane Millot. Ms. Millot has already identified herself. She has testified that she works as a teller at the First National Bank. The prosecution is the proponent.

P	Ms. Millot, WHERE were you on the morning of February 14, 2017? (1)
W	I was at work at the bank.
P	WHAT happened that morning? (1)
W	The bank was robbed.
P	HOW were the robbers dressed? (1)
W	They all had masks on. That's why I can't identify any faces.
P	WHAT happened immediately after the robbers took the money? (1)
W	They made their getaway.
P	HOW did they make their getaway? (1)
W	In a white car parked in front of the bank.
P	WHAT was the car's license number? (1), (5)
W	I can't remember. I saw it, but I can't remember it now.
P	WHAT, if anything, might help you remember? (2)
W	I made a note on a slip of paper I had at the time.
P	WHAT did you note on this slip of paper? (2)
W	The license number of the getaway car.
P	WHO prepared this slip? (3)
W	I did it myself.
P	WHEN did you prepare this slip? (3)
W	Right after the car got away.
P	HOW many minutes passed between the time the car left and the time you wrote on the slip? (3)
W	One or two. Not any more than that. I had the slip of paper at my teller window and a pen in the pocket of my dress.
P	HOW clear was your memory of the license number when you wrote the number down? (3), (4)
W	I don't remember making any mistakes. I looked at it carefully, and it seemed O.K. at the time.
P	Your Honor, I request that this be marked prosecution exhibit number five for identification.
J	It will be so marked.
P	Please let the record reflect that I am showing the exhibit to the opposing counsel.
J	It will so reflect.
P	Ms. Millot, I now hand you prosecution exhibit number five for

identification. WHAT is it?

W	It's the slip of paper I mentioned.
P	HOW can you recognize it?
W	I recognize my handwriting.
P	Please read the exhibit silently to yourself. (*Pause.*) Have you done so?
W	Yes.
P	Now please hand it to me. (*The witness does so.*) Your Honor, please let the record reflect that I am holding the exhibit away from the witness and out of her view.
J	It will so reflect.
P	Ms. Millot, you've had a chance to read the exhibit and refresh your memory. Now, without relying on the exhibit, WHAT was the car's license number? (5)
W	I still can't remember apart from the exhibit.
P	WHY can't you remember? (5)
W	I have a bad memory for numbers. I can't honestly say that I now remember the license number.

In jurisdictions prohibiting the introduction of the exhibit:

Please read the slip of paper to the jury.

W	It reads, "USC 247."
P	WHAT does that stand for?
W	That's the license number of the getaway car.

In jurisdictions permitting the introduction of the exhibit:

P	Your Honor, I now offer prosecution exhibit number five for identification into evidence as prosecution exhibit number five.
J	It will be received.
P	Ms. Millot, please read the exhibit to the jurors.
W	It reads, "USC 247."
P	WHAT does that stand for?
W	It's the license number of the getaway car.

[2] PRESENT RECOLLECTION REFRESHED OR REVIVED

In past recollection recorded, even after viewing the document, the witness cannot recall the relevant fact or event. Suppose that viewing the document refreshed the witness's recollection. Then the witness may testify from his or her revived recollection. The courts use the expressions, "present recollection refreshed" or "present recollection revived" to describe the use of exhibits to refresh present memory. Under this theory, the real evidence is the witness's oral testimony, and the exhibit serves only as a memory aid or jogger. A few courts apply the foundational requirements for past recollection recorded to documents used to refresh recollection. However, most courts draw a clear distinction between the two doctrines and permit the proponent to use any document to refresh recollection. Some courts even broadly permit the proponent to use photographs or songs to revive a witness's memory.

Federal Rule of Evidence 612 governs this practice in federal courts:

> (a)   Scope. This rule gives an adverse party certain options when a witness uses a writing to refresh memory:
>
> > (1)   while testifying; or
>
> > (2)   before testifying, if the court decides that justice requires the party to have those options.
>
> (b)   Adverse Party's Options; Deleting Unrelated Matter. Unless 18 U.S.C. § 3500 provides otherwise in a criminal case, an adverse party is entitled to have the writing produced at the hearing, to inspect it, to cross-examine the witness about it, and to introduce in evidence any portion that relates to the witness's testimony. If the producing party claims that the writing includes unrelated matter, the court must examine the writing in camera, delete any unrelated portion, and order that the rest be delivered to the adverse party. Any portion deleted over objection must be preserved for the record.

If the jurisdiction does not apply the past recollection recorded requirements to present recollection revived, the foundation for present recollection refreshed or revived is quite simple:

1.   The witness states that he or she cannot recall a fact or event.

2.   The witness states that a certain writing or object could help refresh his or her memory. Most jurisdictions do not require this showing as a formal element of the foundation, but many trial attorneys think that it is good practice to have the witness first mention the writing or object.

3.   The proponent tenders the writing or object to the witness.

4.   The proponent asks the witness to silently read the writing or study the object.

5.   The proponent then removes the exhibit from the witness's view.

6.   The witness states that viewing the document or object refreshes his or her memory.

7.   The witness then testifies from revived memory.

On this theory, the evidence is the witness's oral testimony, and the proponent does not formally offer the writing or object into evidence. For purposes of making a good record, many trial judges prefer that the proponent at least mark the writing or object as an exhibit for identification.

We can use the same robbery hypothetical to illustrate present recollection refreshed. In this variation of the hypothetical, Ms. Millot has a better memory for numbers.

P   WHAT was the getaway car's license number? (1)

W	I can't honestly remember right now.
P	WHAT, if anything, might help you remember? (2)
W	I wrote the number down on a slip of paper.
P	Your Honor, I request that this be marked prosecution exhibit number five for identification.
J	It will be so marked.
P	Please let the record reflect that I am showing the exhibit to the opposing counsel.
J	It will so reflect.
P	I request permission to approach the witness.
J	Granted.
P	Ms. Millot, I now hand you prosecution exhibit number five for identification. (3) WHAT is it? (2)
W	It's the slip of paper I mentioned.
P	HOW can you recognize it? (2)
W	I ought to know my own handwriting style.
P	Please read the exhibit silently to yourself. (4) (*Pause.*) Have you done so?
W	Yes.
P	Now hand it to me. (*The witness does so.*) Your Honor, please let the record reflect that I am holding the exhibit away from the witness and out of her view. (5)
J	It will so reflect.
P	Ms. Millot, you've had a chance to read the exhibit to refresh your memory. Now without relying on the exhibit, can you remember the license number? (6)
W	Yes.
P	WHAT was the license number? (7)
W	USC 247.

Many experienced trial attorneys use the following combination of past recollection recorded and present recollection refreshed. As soon as a witness states that he or she cannot recall a fact or event, if possible the proponent lays elements one through four of the past recollection recorded foundation. The proponent then tenders the writing to the witness in an attempt to revive present recollection. If the attempt is successful, the witness testifies from present, refreshed memory. If the attempt is unsuccessful, the witness's inability to recall lays the last element of the past recollection recorded foundation. Questioning the witness in this sequence puts the proponent in a "no loss" situation; whichever response the witness gives, the proponent can elicit the desired testimony.

§ 10.08   LEARNED TREATISES

[1]   THE DOCTRINE

At common law, most jurisdictions permitted the opponent to use a learned text or article to cross-examine an expert witness to impeach the expert. The cross-examiner could confront the expert with a passage that contradicted something that the expert said on direct examination. However, the overwhelming majority of jurisdictions refused to allow an attorney to introduce a passage in a text or article as substantive evidence. For that matter, although a minority of jurisdictions allowed the substantive use of a text or article, even they narrowly limited the scope of the hearsay exception to publications dealing with "exact" sciences such as mathematics and "static" fields such as geography.

The drafters of the Federal Rules both embraced and expanded the scope of the exception. Rule 803(18) currently codifies a hearsay exception for

[a] statement contained in a treatise, periodical, or pamphlet, if:

> (A)   the statement is called to the attention of an expert witness on cross-examination or relied on by the expert on direct examination; and
>
> (B)   the publication is established as a reliable authority by the expert's admission or testimony, by another expert's testimony, or by judicial notice.

If admitted, the statement may be read into evidence but not received as an exhibit.

The original version of Rule 803(18) made it clear that the exception is not confined to texts and articles dealing with "exact" sciences or "static" disciplines; that version of the statute referred to publications "on a subject of history, medicine, or other science or art." The Advisory Committee Note accompanying the 2011 restyling of Rule 803 states that the changed wording was not intended "to change any result in any ruling on evidence admissibility."

While the drafters decided to broaden the scope of the exception, they appreciated the dangers that could arise if texts and articles are used too freely. One danger is that the jury might misinterpret the passage being quoted. After all, the jurors are not experts. For that reason, the rule provides that the passage may be admitted only while an expert is on the stand. The expert's live appearance enables the opponent to question the expert about the meaning of the passage. Another danger is that if the judge sent the text or article into the deliberation room, the jurors could focus on—and misinterpret—other passages. To eliminate that danger, the rule forbids physically submitting the text or article to the jury. The proponent may have the expert quote the passage or, in the judge's discretion, display the passage on, for example, a PowerPoint slide. However, the proponent may not hand the text or article to the jurors for their inspection, and the judge may not send the text or article into the deliberation room.

[2]   ELEMENTS OF THE FOUNDATION

To invoke Rule 803(18), the proponent must lay the following foundation:

1. A witness, qualified as an expert under Rule 702, is on the witness stand.

2. A treatise, periodical, or pamphlet contains a passage dealing with the subject-matter of the expert's testimony.

3. The proponent brings the treatise, periodical, or pamphlet to the expert's attention.

4. The treatise, periodical, or pamphlet has been published.

5. The treatise, periodical, or pamphlet is "a reliable authority" on the subject. This element is fairly liberal. To begin with, the rule recognizes several different methods by which the proponent can establish the publication's reliable status. In a rare case, the text may be so well known that the judge may judicially notice the status under Rule 201(b)(2). Alternatively, based on a prior expert witness's testimony, the proponent may have persuaded the judge to find that the publication is a reliable authority. Finally and more commonly when the text is being used on direct examination, the proponent elicits the witness's testimony to that effect. Moreover, although the proponent must show that in general the publication is reliable, the proponent need not show that the particular passage being quoted has attained authoritative status.

[3] SAMPLE FOUNDATION

The fact situation is a medical malpractice action. The plaintiff alleges that she suffered permanent brain injuries as a result of surgery to remove what the surgeon suspected was a cancerous tumor. It turned out that the tumor was benign. Because of the peculiar location of the tumor in the plaintiff's brain, the surgeon had to use a rare procedure. The plaintiff alleges that the procedure in question has a very high risk of causing brain damage and that to obtain her informed consent, the defendant surgeon should have expressly told her that the procedure posed such a significant danger. The plaintiff contends that if the surgeon had properly warned her, she would not have consented to the surgical procedure that caused her brain injuries. The plaintiff has called Dr. Akhil Seaman. Dr. Seaman initially described his credentials as an expert on brain surgery. Dr. Seaman then expressed his personal opinion that the defendant surgeon violated the standard of care by not specifically telling the plaintiff that the procedure the surgeon contemplated using posed a very significant risk of causing permanent brain damage. The direct examination continues.

P   Dr. Seaman, you've just expressed your personal opinion about the need to warn patients that this procedure poses a substantial risk of causing permanent brain damage. WHAT texts, if any, in your field, discuss this topic? (2)

W   The leading text is Welby on *Modern Brain Surgery*, sixth edition, 2016.

P   WHO publishes the text? (4)

W   As I recall, the publisher is Medical Books in Chicago.

P   HOW long has this text been in publication? (4), (5)

W   I've had the text in my personal library since the first edition came out

	in 2002. It's now in a sixth, 2016 edition.
P	WHO is the author of the text? (5)
W	Dr. Susan Welby.
P	WHO is Dr. Welby? (5)
W	She's one of the leading brain surgeons in the world. She's currently the head of the brain surgery department at the medical school of The Johns Hopkins University, one of the most respected medical schools in the world. She's been a president of both national and international organizations of surgeons.
P	HOW well regarded in her text, *Modern Brain Surgery*? (5)
W	It's one of the standard, pre-eminent texts in the field. I teach at our local medical school, and I have always assigned the text as a required reading in my course. I believe it's the most widely used text on brain surgery at American medical schools. Moreover, it's frequently widely cited as authority in articles by other surgeons. In my last article, I included several citations to the text.
P	Does Dr. Welby's text discuss the procedure that the defendant doctor used in this case? (2)
W	It most certainly does. There's a very detailed discussion of the topic in Chapter 13 of the sixth edition.
P	In particular, does the text discuss the warnings needed to obtain truly informed consent to the procedure? (2)
W	Yes.
P	Your Honor, I request that this be marked plaintiff's exhibit number seven for identification.
W	It will be so marked.
P	Your Honor, please let the record reflect that I am showing the exhibit to the defense counsel.
W	The record will so reflect.
P	Permission to approach the witness?
W	Granted.
P	Dr. Seaman, I now hand you what has been marked as plaintiff's exhibit number seven for identification. Do you recognize it? (2)
W	Of course.
P	WHAT is it? (2)
W	It's the latest, sixth edition of Dr. Welby's book.
P	HOW do you recognize it? (2)
W	I recognize both the cover and, quickly browsing through the book, the

contents as well. As I said, I have this edition in my personal library. In fact, it sits on my desk, and I regularly consult it.

P   Your Honor, I now request the admission of the first full paragraph on page 367 of the exhibit?

J   Any objection?

O   Yes. Your Honor, he can't introduce the text.

       Do you wish to be heard before I rule?

P   Yes, Your Honor, the statute expressly says "[i]f admitted." The statute obviously authorizes me to admit the text and read a relevant passage to the jury. It simply forbids me from handing the text to the jury; the statute says it cannot be physically "received." I'm not asking for permission to hand the text to the jury. All I want Dr. Seaman to do is read that passage to the jurors.

J   Objection overruled. Permission granted.

P   Thank you, Your Honor. Dr. Seaman, please read the first full paragraph on page 367 to the ladies and gentlemen of the jury.

§ 10.09   EXCITED OR STARTLED UTTERANCES

[1]   THE DOCTRINE

In the last three sections, we analyzed documentary hearsay exceptions resting primarily on a showing of reliability. In each case, the showing is based on testimony describing the trustworthy manner in which the document was generated. The next four sections address other hearsay exceptions recognized principally because of an inference of reliability. In these exceptions, however, the inference of reliability has a different basis; each exception in this category is a variation of the ancient *res gestae* doctrine and rests on an inference of the declarant's sincerity. This category includes excited utterances, present sense impressions, declarations of bodily condition, and statements of mental condition.

The exception for excited utterances illustrates the common rationale of the exceptions in this category. A startling event occurs, an observer becomes excited, and the observer then makes a spontaneous statement about the event. The statement's spontaneity is the circumstantial guarantee of the declarant's sincerity. Federal Rule of Evidence 803(2) describes the doctrine in this fashion: "The following [is] not excluded by the rule against hearsay . . .: A statement relating to a startling event or condition, made while the declarant was under the stress of excitement that it caused."

[2]   ELEMENTS OF THE FOUNDATION

The foundation for an excited utterance includes the following elements:

1.   An event occurred. Many jurisdictions, including the federal courts, do not require any independent, corroborating evidence that the event occurred; these courts accept the declarant's assertion of the event's occurrence at face value. A minority of jurisdictions requires independent evidence as part of the

foundation. However, even in these jurisdictions, the quantum of required corroboration is usually slight. For example, if the declaration refers to an assault on the declarant and, at the time, the declarant's clothing was dirty and disheveled, the declarant's appearance might be sufficient corroboration that the assault occurred.

2. The event was startling, or at least stressful. This element is the objective guarantee of the statement's sincerity. The nature of the event was likely to inspire stress or nervous excitement.

3. The declarant had personal knowledge of the event. The declarant must have been a participant in or observer of the event. Again, the courts apply this element laxly. In some cases, the declarants have been unidentified bystanders. The courts have admitted the bystanders' excited statements so long as the time and place of the statement suggest that the bystander actually observed the event. Thus, if a person made a statement a few minutes after an accident and at the same intersection where the accident occurred, the court might well assume that the declarant observed the accident.

4. The declarant made a statement about the event. At the end of the foundational questioning, the proponent usually asks the witness whether the out-of-court declarant made a statement "about" the event. Some courts have relaxed this requirement. In *United States v. Napier*, 518 F.2d 316 (9th Cir. 1975), a kidnapping victim was injured and became unconscious. Weeks later she saw a newspaper article containing a photograph of the defendant. She immediately stated, "He killed me, he killed me." The court admitted the statement as evidence of the defendant's identity as the kidnapper. Some state courts are following suit and accepting so-called "re-excited" utterances.[2] This trend is dubious, since the assertions relate to the earlier event and the time lapse can be so significant that there are grave doubts about the quality of the declarant's memory. Nevertheless, this trend is emerging.

5. The declarant made the statement while he or she was in a state of nervous excitement. This element is the subjective guarantee of the statement's sincerity.

[3] SAMPLE FOUNDATION

Our fact situation is a tort action arising from a collision at an intersection. The plaintiff was driving a blue car. The defendant was driving a red car. The issue is which car was facing and ran a red light. The plaintiff calls Mr. Reynolds as a witness. Mr. Reynolds has already identified himself. The plaintiff is the proponent.

P   WHERE were you on the afternoon of March 13, 2017? (1)

---

[2] Carolyn B. Tapie, Comment, *The Crying Game: How* Hunt v. State *Unnecessarily Expands the Definition of an Excited Utterance in Texas*, 56 BAYLOR L. REV. 723, 724–725 (2004) (under the state version of Rule 803(2), some courts admit statements about crimes even when the statement was prompted by a later exciting event such as a movie depicting a similar crime).

W	I was in downtown Jefferson City at the intersection of Cedar Street and Sixth Avenue.
P	WHY were you there? (1)
W	I just happened to be walking my dog.
P	WHAT, if anything, happened at the intersection while you were there? (1), (2)
W	There was a collision.
P	HOW noisy was the collision? (1), (2)
W	It was an awful, shattering sound.
P	HOW many bystanders were there? (1)
W	I'd say that there were about 20 people in the immediate vicinity.
P	WHAT was their reaction to the collision? (2)
W	We were all shocked. It happened so fast, and the noise was so loud. And as soon as we looked, we could see that some people were injured and bleeding. It was just an awful sight.
P	WHO else besides yourself was in the crowd of bystanders? (3)
W	There were a number of people mingling around, but there was one guy in particular who stuck in my mind.
P	WHAT was his name? (3)
W	I never got his name.
P	WHAT did he look like?
W	He was a male Caucasian, maybe 30 or 35.
P	WHERE was he at the time of the collision? (3)
W	Standing right next to me.
P	HOW was he facing? (3)
W	He was looking right into the intersection. He was evidently waiting for the light to change to walk across.
P	WHAT was his condition right after the collision? (5)
W	He was just like the rest of us—shocked and frightened.
	WHAT was his facial expression? (5)
W	He had his mouth open—I guess he was dumbfounded at first.
P	WHAT was his tone of voice? (5)
W	He was shouting in a loud voice.
W	WHAT were his gestures? (5)
W	He was pointing at the wreck and gesturing wildly. He was very animated.

P	WHAT, if anything, did he say about the accident? (6)
O	Your Honor, I object to that question on the ground that it calls for hearsay.
P	Your Honor, may I be heard?
J	Yes.
P	Although the statement is hearsay, it pretty clearly falls within the excited utterance exception.
J	I agree. The objection will be overruled.
P	Mr. Reynolds, let me repeat the question. WHAT, if anything, did this man say about the accident? (4)
W	He said that the fellow in the red car had gone right through the red light and caused the collision.

§ 10.10   PRESENT SENSE IMPRESSIONS OR CONTEMPORANEOUS STATEMENTS

[1]   THE DOCTRINE

The spontaneity of the statement is the basic rationale for the excited utterance exception. The statement's contemporaneity can also serve as proof of the statement's trustworthiness. Misrecollection is one of the most common causes of testimonial error, and the fact that the declarant makes the statement at roughly the same time the event occurs is some evidence of the statement's reliability. A growing number of courts accept the contemporaneous statement or present sense impression doctrine as a separate hearsay exception. The federal courts joined ranks with those courts when Congress enacted Federal Rule of Evidence 803(1): "The following [is] not excluded by the rule against hearsay . . .: A statement describing or explaining an event or condition, made while or immediately after the declarant perceived it."

The present sense impression doctrine differs from the excited utterance doctrine in three important respects. First, the timing requirement is more rigorous under the present sense impression doctrine. To qualify as a contemporaneous statement, the declaration must usually be made within minutes after the event. If the declarant is still excited or in pain, an excited utterance can be made hours after the event. Second, the event need not be startling to prompt a present sense impression statement. The guarantee of trustworthiness is contemporaneity rather than nervous spontaneity. Finally, in some jurisdictions such as California, contemporaneous statements are limited to statements describing or explaining the declarant's own conduct. A declarant may make an excited utterance about any startling, external event; but in a minority of jurisdictions, a present sense impression must relate to the declarant's own conduct. In these jurisdictions, the statement must describe, explain, or qualify the declarant's acts.

[2]   ELEMENTS OF THE FOUNDATION

The foundation for present sense impression includes these elements:

1. An event occurred. As in the case of excited utterances, there is a split of

authority whether the proponent must present independent, corroborating evidence that the event occurred.

2. The declarant had personal knowledge of the event.

3. The declarant made the statement during or very shortly after the event. While an acceptable delay under Rule 803(2) is often measured in terms of hours, under Rule 803(1) the delay is usually measured in terms of seconds or minutes.

4. The statement describes or explains the event. As previously stated, a minority of jurisdictions follows a more restrictive approach. These jurisdictions insist that the declaration relate to the declarant's own conduct. Many courts construe the "describing or explaining" language in Rule 803(1) more narrowly than the "relating to" wording in Rule 803(2).

5. In some jurisdictions, the witness on the stand must have observed the same event—the percipient witness limitation. This element ensures that a witness is available to verify or contradict the declaration. The modern statutes codifying the present sense impression doctrine usually omit this requirement. For example, the text of Federal Rule of Evidence 803(1) makes no mention of this requirement. However, some commentators have pointed out that the Advisory Committee Note to Rule 803 cites many of the older writings about the present sense impression doctrine advocating the percipient witness limitation. More-over, the Note contains a passage which seemingly assumes compliance with the limitation: "If the witness is not the declarant, he may be examined as to the circumstances as an aid in evaluating the statement." Given that Note, several courts enforce the percipient witness limitation; and while they stop short of embracing the limitation, other courts require corroboration. See the discussion of element #1, *supra*.

[3] SAMPLE FOUNDATION

To illustrate this doctrine, we can use the same hypothetical as in § 10.08. In this variation of the hypothetical, the proponent deletes the questions designed to show the declarant's nervous excitement.

P	WHERE were you on the afternoon of March 13, 2017? (1), (5)
W	I was in downtown Jefferson City at the intersection of Cedar Street and Sixth Avenue.
P	WHY were you there? (1), (5)
W	I just happened to be walking my dog there.
P	WHAT, if anything, happened at the intersection while you were there? (1), (5)
W	There was a collision.
P	HOW far were you from the collision when it occurred? (1), (5)
W	I was about 30 feet from the point of impact. That's just a rough estimate.

P	HOW were you facing? (1), (5)
W	I was waiting for the light to change, so I was looking right into the intersection.
P	HOW clear was your line of sight to the collision? (1), (5)
W	It was clear. I don't think there were any cars obstructing my view.
	HOW much of the collision did you see? (1), (5)
W	Just about the whole thing. I saw the cars approaching the intersection and actually collide.
P	HOW many other bystanders were there? (2)
W	I'd say that there were about 20 people in the immediate vicinity.
P	WHO were the bystanders? (2)
W	I didn't know any by name, but one guy in particular stuck in my mind.
P	WHAT did he look like? (2)
W	He was a male African-American, maybe 30 or 35.
P	WHERE was he at the time of the collision? (2)
W	He was standing right next to me.
P	HOW was he facing? (2)
W	He was looking right into the intersection. He was evidently waiting for the light to change to walk across.
P	WHAT did he do after the collision? (3)
W	He was pointing to the wreck, and we talked about the collision.
P	WHEN did you and this bystander talk about the collision? (3)
W	Right after it.
P	HOW many minutes elapsed between the collision and your discussion of the collision with this bystander? (3)
W	It may have taken us a minute or two to get over the shock of what we had witnessed, but it was no longer than that.
P	WHAT, if anything, did this bystander say about the accident? (4)
O	Your Honor, I object to that question on the ground that it calls for hearsay.
P	Your Honor, may I be heard?
J	Yes.
P	I will concede that the question calls for hearsay, but the record shows that any statement by the bystander qualifies as a present sense impression or contemporaneous statement.

In most jurisdictions:

J	The objection will be overruled.
P	Mr. Reynolds, let me repeat the question. WHAT, if anything, did this bystander say about the accident? (4)
W	He said that the fellow in the red car had gone right through the red light and caused the collision.

In the minority of jurisdictions restricting present sense impressions to statements describing the declarant's own conduct:

O	It's true that the statement was roughly contemporaneous with the event. However, as Your Honor knows, this jurisdiction limits present sense impressions to statements describing the declarant's own conduct. The bystander was describing an external event, the collision, rather than his own conduct.
J	Objection sustained.

§ 10.11 DECLARATIONS OF STATE OF MIND OR EMOTION

[1] OFFERED TO PROVE STATE OF MIND OR EMOTION

One of the most difficult things for a trial attorney to prove is a person's state of mind. The attorney must usually rely on circumstantial proof such as conduct that evidences a certain state of mind. However, sometimes a person openly asserts his or her state of mind. Because of the difficulty of proving state of mind, the courts have been especially eager to admit any evidently sincere declarations of state of mind or emotion. These declarations often give us the best insight into the declarant's state of mind or emotion. Thus, the courts have developed a general rule that these declarations are admissible; if a person declares his or her then existing state of mind or emotion, the declaration is admissible to prove the existence of that state of mind or emotion. Federal Rule of Evidence 803(3) provides: "The following [is] not excluded by the rule against hearsay . . .: A statement of the declarant's then existing state of mind (such as motive, intent, or plan) or emotional . . . condition (such as mental feeling)."

Ideally, the declarant will make the statement at the pivotal time under the substantive law. For example, under Real Property law, the grantor must have the intent to pass title when handing the deed to the grantee. If at the very instant of handing the deed to the grantee, the grantor announces the intent to pass title, the statement is certainly admissible. What if the grantor makes such a statement shortly before or shortly after the manual delivery of the deed? The courts still admit the statement on the theory of continuity of state of mind; there are no intervening events that would plausibly change the person's frame of mind, and the time lapse between the statement and the critical event is so short that we may reasonably assume that the declarant's state of mind was the same at both times.

The foundation for this doctrine is simple. The making of the statement by the declarant is an event. The proponent need establish only the normal foundation for an event:

1. Where the statement was made.

2. When the statement was made. The declarant must make the statement at or near the pivotal time under the substantive law.

3. Who was present.

4. Who made the statement.

5. The tenor of the statement.

Our fact situation is a quiet title action. The plaintiff, Ms. Sheila Morris, has brought suit against the defendant, Ms. Marilyn Winters. Ms. Morris claims title from the original titleholder, Mr. Forest Morris, her grandfather. She claims that on December 25, 2016, her grandfather gave her a deed to the property as a Christmas present. The plaintiff calls Mr. Thomas Morris, her brother, as a witness. The plaintiff is the proponent.

P   WHERE were you on December 25, 2016? (1), (2)

W   I was at our family Christmas party at Camden.

P   WHO else was there? (3)

W   All the close relatives, including Grandfather and my sister, Sheila.

P   WHAT, if anything, unusual happened during the party?

W   As an unexpected Christmas gift, Grandfather handed Sheila a deed to our land in Vermont.

P   WHAT, if anything, did he do when he handed her the deed? (4)

W   Well, he did say something.

P   WHAT did he say? (5)

W   He said that he wanted her to have the land because, ever since she was a little girl, she had loved to vacation there.

In the next variation of the hypothetical, the grantor makes the statement shortly before delivery of the deed.

P   WHERE were you on December 25th, 2016? (1), (2)

W   I was at our family Christmas party at Camden.

P   WHO else was there? (3)

W   All the close relatives, including Grandfather and my sister, Sheila.

P   WHAT, if anything, unusual happened during the party?

W   As an unexpected Christmas gift, Grandfather handed Sheila a deed to our land in Vermont.

P   WHAT, if anything, did he say about the deed during the party? (5)

O   Objection, Your Honor. That question calls for hearsay.

P   Your Honor, may we approach the bench?

J   Yes.

P   Your Honor, I offer to prove that the witness will say the Grandfather said he wanted Sheila to have the land. The witness will also testify the Grandfather made this statement only an hour before handing the deed to Sheila. The time lapse is so short that we may assume that the Grandfather's state of mind was the same at both times.

J   The objection will be overruled.

P   Mr. Morris, let me repeat the question. WHAT, if anything, did your Grandfather say about the deed during the party? (5)

W   He said he wanted Sheila to have the land because, ever since she was a little girl, she had loved to vacation there.

P   WHEN did your Grandfather say that? (4)

W   A little while before he handed the deed to her.

P   Specifically, HOW many minutes or hours before he handed her the deed? (4)

W   About an hour—maybe a little less.

[2] OFFERED TO PROVE SUBSEQUENT CONDUCT

In § 10.10[1], we use declarations of state of mind when state of mind itself is in issue. There is another use for state of mind declarations. Suppose that the declaration is a statement of present plan, intention, or design: "I plan to," "I intend to," or "I am going to." These declarations indicate that the declarant currently plans to engage in subsequent conduct. Moreover, the fact that the declarant expressed that intent increases the probability that the declarant subsequently performed the planned act. Federal Rule of Evidence 803(3) also sanctions this use of state of mind declarations; it expressly authorizes the admission of statements of "intent, . . . or plan."

The foundation is the same as in § 10.10[1]:

1. Where the statement was made.
2. When the statement was made.
3. Who was present.
4. Who made the statement.
5. The tenor of the statement.

The fact situation is a burglary prosecution. The government alleges that the accused, Mr. Michael Waylen, burglarized a drug store in Tulsa on August 17, 2017. The defendant has raised an alibi defense. The defendant testified that he was with his girlfriend in Oklahoma City on the day of the burglary. His girlfriend testified to the same effect. Now the defendant calls Mr. John Farmer as a witness. Mr. Farmer has already identified himself. The defendant is the proponent:

P   Mr. Farmer, WHERE were you on the evening of August 15, 2017? (1), (2)

W   I was at a party at a friend's here in Tulsa.

P   WHO else was at the party?

W	A lot of people, including the accused, Michael Waylen.
P	WHERE is the accused now? (3)
W	He's in the courtroom.
P	Specifically, WHERE in the courtroom? (3)
W	He's sitting at that table.
P	HOW is he dressed? (3)
W	He's wearing a gray sweater and black pants.
P	Your Honor, please let the record reflect that the witness has identified the accused.
J	It will so reflect.
P	Mr. Farmer, WHAT happened during the party? (4)
W	It was just a quiet party. I drank a little and talked with some friends.
P	WHOM did you talk with? (4)
W	I had a nice long talk with Michael, the accused. We sat together near a coffee table.
P	WHAT did you talk about? (5)
W	A lot of things, especially his plans for the future.
P	WHAT, if anything, did the accused say about his immediate plans? (5)
O	Your Honor, I object to that last question on the ground that it calls for self-serving hearsay.
P	Your Honor, may we approach the bench to be heard?
J	Yes.
P	Your Honor, I offer to prove that the witness will testify that the accused said he intended to visit his girlfriend in Oklahoma City the weekend of the alleged crime. The accused's statement falls within the hearsay exception for declarations of present state of mind.
J	The objection will be overruled. You may proceed.
P	WHAT, if anything, did the accused say about his immediate plans? (5)
W	He said that that weekend he was going to visit his girlfriend, Norma, in Oklahoma City.
P	WHICH weekend was he referring to? (5)
W	He mentioned the weekend of August 17 and 18.

Assume that a murder victim made a statement that she presently intended to meet the accused at a particular location. Later the victim's body is found at that location. Under this exception, the victim's statement is certainly admissible to prove that she carried out her plan and went to that location. Is the statement also admissible as evidence that the accused met her at that location? The courts have long divided over that question. There is a strong argument that the evidence is inadmissible for that purpose. The courts ordinarily do not allow one witness to directly speculate as to another person's state of mind;[3] without more facts, the judge would have barred the declarant from testifying on the witness stand that the accused shared her plan and intention,[4] If the jurisdiction holds that the statement is inadmissible for that purpose, the judge must either redact the reference to the accused or give the jury a limiting instruction about the proper use of the statement. In the limiting instruction, the judge would tell the jury that although they could treat the statement as the basis for an inference as to the declarant's own later conduct, they could not use the statement as evidence of the accused's conduct. Thus, in closing argument the prosecutor could employ the statement as evidence that the declarant went to the location she mentioned, but the prosecutor could not utilize the statement as evidence that the accused went to that location.

§ 10.12 DECLARATIONS OF BODILY CONDITION

[1] PRESENT BODILY CONDITION

The courts are almost as willing to admit evidently sincere statements of bodily condition as they are to admit statements of mental condition. Federal Rule of Evidence 803(3) specifically authorizes the admission of statements of "sensory . . . or physical condition (such as . . . pain . . . or bodily health)." Ordinarily, if a declarant proclaims his or her present bodily sensation or condition, the declaration is admissible. However, many courts exclude statements made to a physician who was consulted solely to qualify the physician to testify at trial.

The foundation includes these elements:

1. Where the statement was made.

2. When the statement was made.

3. Who was present.

4. Who made the statement.

5. Whom the statement was made to. The statement can be made to a lay person or a physician. The traditional, common-law view is that the statement may not be made to a physician consulted solely for purposes of trial testimony. However, the Federal Rules abandon that view.

6. The tenor of the statement. The statement must refer to the person's present bodily condition.

This fact situation will illustrate the doctrine. The plaintiff, Ms. Joan Gillette, brings a product liability action against Miller Pharmaceuticals. The plaintiff alleges that the

---

[3] However, as § 9.02[2] points out, Rule 701 permits a lay witness to opine about a third party's "apparent" or "seeming" state of mind if the opinion is based on the witness's observation of the third party's demeanor.

[4] If the accused stated their plan to the declarant, the accused's statement would fall within 803(3). However, at trial the proponent ordinarily cannot prove that the accused made such a statement.

defendant sold her defective medication and that the medication caused her serious internal injuries. Her complaint prayed for $20,000 for pain and suffering. At the trial, she called Mr. Leonard Wright as a witness. Mr. Wright identifies himself and states that he is a physician. The plaintiff is the proponent.

P	Doctor Wright, WHERE were you on the afternoon of January 28, 2017? (1), (2)
W	In my office.
P	WHO else was there? (3)
W	The plaintiff, Ms. Gillette.
P	WHERE is the plaintiff now? (3)
W	In this courtroom.
P	Specifically, WHERE in the courtroom? (3)
W	She's sitting at that table to your right.
P	HOW is she dressed? (3)
W	She's wearing a white blouse and a green skirt.
P	Your Honor, please let the record reflect that the witness identified the plaintiff.
J	It will so reflect.
P	WHAT happened while the plaintiff was at your office? (3)
W	I examined her.
P	WHAT, if anything, did she say to you about her physical condition during the examination? (4), (5), (6)
O	Your Honor, I object to that question on the ground that it calls for hearsay.
P	Your Honor, may we approach the bench?
J	Yes.
P	I concede that the question calls for hearsay. However, I offer to prove that the witness will testify that the plaintiff said she was then in terrible pain. That statement qualifies as a declaration of present bodily condition.
O	Your Honor, I request permission to take the witness on voir dire before you rule on my objection.
J	Permission granted.
O	Doctor Wright, ISN'T IT TRUE THAT you didn't give the plaintiff any medicine during this examination?
W	Yes.
O	ISN'T IT A FACT THAT the plaintiff never asked you for medication?

	(5)
W	Yes.
O	ISN'T IT TRUE THAT you never prescribed any treatment for her? (5)
W	Yes.
O	AND ISN'T IT CORRECT THAT the plaintiff told you that she was consulting you so that you could testify at this trial? (5)
W	Yes.
O	Your Honor, I renew my objection. It's clear that Dr. Wright is a physician consulted solely for purposes of testimony. The hearsay exception is inapplicable.
J	The objection will be sustained.

The above ruling would be proper under the traditional, common-law rule forbidding the receipt of statements to physicians consulted solely for purposes of trial preparation. However, as previously stated, that ruling would be erroneous under the Federal Rules.

[2] PAST BODILY CONDITION

A majority of jurisdictions now admit statements of past bodily condition as substantive proof in limited circumstances. The Federal Rules commit the federal courts to this view. Federal Rule of Evidence 803(4) states: "The following [is] not excluded by the rule against hearsay . . .: A statement that: (A) is made for—and is reasonably pertinent to—medical diagnosis or treatment; and (B) describes medical history; past or present symptoms or sensations; their inception; or their general cause." Thus, the rule requires a showing of both the declarant's subjective medical motivation and the objective pertinence of the declaration to medical diagnosis or treatment.

In the common-law jurisdictions admitting declarations of past bodily condition, the foundation usually includes these elements:

1. The declarant made the statement to a proper addressee. Many jurisdictions limit this exception to statements made to physicians. The Federal Rules do not contain that limitation. The Advisory Committee's Note to Rule 803 states that the exception encompasses statements made to "hospital attendants, ambulance drivers, or even members of the family." Such statements are admissible so long as the other foundational elements are satisfied—for instance, when the declarant makes a statement to a hospital attendant to be relayed to a treating physician.

2. The declarant made the statement for a medical motive. This element relates to the declarant's subjective motivation for making the statement. At common law, most jurisdictions subscribing to this exception require that the declarant have a significant treatment motive; it is insufficient if the declarant is consulting a physician to testify at trial. The Federal Rules opt for a more liberal view. The Rules permit the statement's admission if the declarant sought "medical diagnosis or treatment." Given the alternative wording of the rule, a diagnosis for purpose of trial is sufficient. The Advisory Committee

Note expressly repudiates the "[c]onventional doctrine . . . exclud(ing) from the hearsay exception, as not within its guarantee of truthfulness, statements to a physician consulted only for the purpose of enabling him to testify." In most cases, the declarant entertaining the medical motive is the potential patient. However, in a number of cases in which the potential patient was unconscious or very seriously injured, the courts have treated family members or even bystanders as proper declarants so long as their evident motive was to provide information relevant to the treatment of the potential patient.

3. The subject-matter of the statement was proper. Most jurisdictions recognizing the exception limit its scope to statements of past bodily condition. Once again, the Federal Rules adopt a broader view. Rule 803(4) also authorizes the admission of statements of the "inception . . . or general cause" of a physical condition. The Advisory Committee's Note contains this explanatory language: "Statements as to fault would not ordinarily qualify under this latter language. Thus a patient's statement that he was struck by an automobile would qualify but not his statement that the car was driven through a red light." Hence, a general reference to an external cause is admissible, but a statement specifically attributing fault to a person will probably be excluded.

4. The content of the statement was objectively pertinent to medical diagnosis or treatment. Rule 803(4) uses the language, "reasonably pertinent." As previously stated, the declarant's subjective motivation is not only relevant but also a requirement. See element #2. However, the rule demands a further circumstantial guarantee of reliability. From a hypothetical reasonable doctor's perspective, the information disclosed in the statement must be pertinent to diagnosis or treatment.

Our fact situation is a personal injury action. The plaintiff, Ms. Norton, alleges that she sustained severe internal injuries after drinking some of the defendant's medicine. The defendant is Shavers Drug Company. The plaintiff wants to introduce a hospital record. The record contains the following entry in section #15 Medical History: "The patient stated she experienced intense pain after drinking from a bottle of cough medicine." The plaintiff calls Mr. Florence as a witness. Mr. Florence identifies himself, states that he is University Hospital's records librarian, and lays a proper business entry foundation for the hospital record itself. The exhibit has already been marked for identification as plaintiff's exhibit number four. The plaintiff is the proponent.

P   Now, doctor, permit me to direct your attention to this section on exhibit #4 for identification, the section labeled #15. WHAT is that section?

W   That's the case history part of the patient's record.

P   WHAT is case history?

W   The patient's past medical history.

P   WHO took this medical history? (1)

W   Dr. Morrell, one of our internists.

P   HOW do you know he took it? (1)

W	I recognize his signature and handwriting style.
P	WHO normally takes the history? (1)
W	The physician who's the intern.
P	WHEN does the intern ordinarily take the history from the patient? (2)
W	As soon as the patient arrives at the first processing station.
P	WHY does the intern take the history? (2), (4)
W	It's often critical to diagnosis and treatment. The case history helps you make a much more informed evaluation of the patient's condition.
P	WHAT, if anything, does the intern usually tell the patient about the purpose of taking the case history? (2)
W	Some patients are very resentful of prying, and we always tell them that we are taking the history to give them better treatment. We tell them we need to know everything about their medical past.
P	Now, doctor, without disclosing to the jury the precise entry on the exhibit, WHY would this particular entry have been included in the patient's case history? (2), (4)
W	Well, it describes how the patient suffered the injuries. The treating doctor has to have that sort of data to do a professional, competent job.
P	Your Honor, I now offer plaintiff's exhibit number four for identification into evidence as plaintiff's exhibit number four.
O	Your Honor, I object to the introduction of the exhibit on the ground that it is hearsay. In fact, it is double hearsay.
P	Your Honor, may we approach the bench?
J	Yes.
P	Your Honor, even double hearsay is admissible if each statement falls within a hearsay exception. The first statement, the hospital record itself, qualifies as a business entry.
J	Are we in agreement on that point?
O	Yes, Your Honor.
P	The second statement, of course, is my client's statement reflected in section #15 of the report. I feel that it qualifies as a statement of past bodily condition. My client had a subjective motivation to be truthful; my client made the statement to a physician for a treatment motive. Moreover, as Mr. Florence's testimony indicates, this information was objectively pertinent to diagnosis or treatment. In this jurisdiction, in such circumstances statements of past condition and external cause are admissible.
J	The objection will be overruled, and the exhibit will be received.

P   Doctor Florence, would you please read section #15 to the jury?

W   It reads: "The patient stated she experienced intense pain after drinking from a bottle of cough medicine." (3)

[3]   EXTERNAL CAUSE OR SOURCE

As the preceding subsection pointed out, Federal Rule of Evidence 803(4) permits the admission of statements describing the "inception . . . or general cause" of the physical condition. The drafters undoubtedly contemplated that this exception would be used primarily in civil cases. However, numerous jurisdictions have utilized the exception in criminal cases as well. In particular, many courts have extended the exception in child abuse prosecutions to justify admitting the child's pretrial statement identifying the abuser. In *White v. Illinois*, 502 U.S. 346, 112 S. Ct. 736, 116 L. Ed. 2d 848 (1992), the Supreme Court rejected a confrontation clause challenge to the extension.

Although there is a large body of case law approving this application of the exception, several courts have stated that the exception must be used with "great caution." For that reason, the proponent must ensure that he or she lays a satisfactory foundation. A complete foundation would include these elements:

1.   The person who made the statement was a proper declarant. In the typical case, the declarant is the patient. However, if the patient is unconscious or unavailable, a relative, friend, or even a Good Samaritan bystander may be the declarant who provides the information to the medical personnel.

2.   The declarant made the statement to a proper addressee. All courts agree that physicians (including psychiatrists) and clinical psychologists are proper addressees. Some courts also admit statements made to social workers. Most courts would likely balk at invoking this exception to uphold the admission of a statement made to a high school guidance counselor.

3.   The declarants knew that the person they were speaking with was a proper addressee. In one case, the court excluded the statement for the stated reason that there was no foundational showing that the child knew that the addressee was a physician. The addressee's statements to the child, identifying the addressee's occupation, would be admissible for the nonhearsay purpose under Rule 801(c)(2); the statements are relevant as mental input to show their effect on the child's state of mind, namely, placing the child on notice of the addressee's occupation.

4.   The declarant made the statement for a medical motive, either treatment or diagnosis. This subjective motivation indicates that the declarant was being truthful. As in the case of element #2, the addressee's statements to the child, identifying the purpose of the meeting, are admissible for a nonhearsay purpose under Rule 801(c)(2). Moreover, the child's statements, declaring his or her purpose in seeking assistance, qualify for admission under Rule 803(3).

5.   The particular statement offered was medically relevant in an objective sense. The language of Rule 803(4) confines the scope of the exception to statements

"reasonably pertinent to . . . medical diagnosis or treatment." The addressee should explain why the particular detail in question could affect either the diagnosis or treatment. In a child abuse prosecution, the detail of the perpetrator's identity arguably possesses both diagnostic and therapeutic relevance. If the child has been victimized by a family member rather than a complete stranger, the symptomatology will be somewhat different. Moreover, when the abuser is a family member, the therapy can differ radically; effective treatment may necessitate the child's removal from the home environment.

6.   The declarant, for example a child, realized that the statement was medically relevant. In his lead opinion in *White*, Chief Justice Rehnquist focused on the inference of sincerity which arises from the fact that "the declarant knows that a false statement can cause misdiagnosis or mistreatment." One of the leading treatises took the position that the statement should be admissible under Rule 803(4) so long as this foundational element is present even if "the . . . physician viewed the matter as irrelevant." 4 DAVID W. LOUISELL & CHRISTOPHER B. MUELLER, FEDERAL EVIDENCE § 444, at 598 (1980). The authors of the successor treatise argue that the subjective understanding of the speaker should be determinative. 4 CHRISTOPHER B. MUELLER & LAIRD C. KIRKPATRICK, FEDERAL EVIDENCE § 8:75 (4th ed. 2013). However, the language of restyled Rule 803(4)(A) appears to resolve the issue; according to the revised wording, the statement must both be "made for . . . medical diagnosis or treatment" "and" be "reasonably pertinent to . . . medical diagnosis or treatment." As in the case of elements #2 and #3, the addressee's statements to the child are admissible nonhearsay under Rule 801(c)(2); and the child's statements reflecting the realization can qualify for admission under Rule 803(3).

The fact situation is a child abuse prosecution. The accused is Paul Leslie. The indictment alleges that the accused sexually abused his minor son Walter. The prosecution calls Dr. Kevin Amar as its next witness.

P	Please state your full name and spell your last name for the record.
W	My name is Kevin Amar. My surname is spelled A - M - A - R.
P	Mr. Amar, WHERE do you live?
W	I live right here in Colorado Springs.
P	WHAT is your occupation? (2)
W	I am a licensed physician and psychiatrist in this state.
P	WHAT is your educational background? (2)
W	I received my M.D. degree from the University of Texas. I then did my internship at U.S.C. Medical Center. I next spent three years as a resident in psychiatry in New York. I have specialized in pediatric psychiatry.
P	WHERE were you on the afternoon of November 12th of last year?
W	I was in my office in Colorado Springs.

P	WHAT happened that afternoon at your office? (1)
W	That was the afternoon when the social worker, Ms. Lucey, brought Walter Leslie by my office.
P	WHERE is Walter right now? (1)
W	He's in the courtroom. He's sitting in the first row of the spectators' area of the courtroom.
P	HOW is he dressed? (1)
W	He's wearing a blue suit, white shirt, and green tie.
P	Your Honor, please let the record reflect that the witness has identified Walter Leslie, the alleged victim in this case. (1)
J	The record will so reflect.
P	Doctor Amar, when Walter arrived, HOW did you identify yourself to him? (3)
W	I told him that I was Doctor Amar and that I was going to talk to him to see if I could help him.
P	During the balance of this meeting, HOW did he refer to you? (3)
W	He called me either "Doctor Amar" or "Doctor."
P	After you identified yourself, WHAT did you tell him about the purpose of your interview with him? (4)
W	I told him that I wanted to talk to him to see if I could help him. I told him that I heard that he was having some emotional problems, and I wanted to see if I could help him overcome those problems.
P	WHAT, if anything, did he say about his reason for coming to see you? (4)
W	He said that Ms. Lucey had told him that I was a doctor and he had agreed to visit me to obtain some medical advice about his problems.

(During this part of the direct examination, the prosecutor would elicit Walter's statements generally describing both his emotional problems and the abuse which caused the problems. The direct examination continues.)

P	WHAT, if anything, did you ask Walter about the identity of the person who abused him? (5)
W	I asked him point-blank who did it.
P	WHY did you do that? (5)
W	I needed to know that for both diagnostic and therapeutic purposes.
P	Please be more specific. HOW could the identity of the abuser affect your diagnosis in Walter's case? (5)
W	Well, to confirm a diagnosis, you need to review the case history to see

if it contains an indication of symptoms appropriate for that diagnosis. When the abuser is a family member—someone the child has trusted and then betrayed the child—you expect somewhat different symptoms than those you encounter when the child is abused by a stranger. In the latter case, abuse by a stranger, you may find a phobia about leaving the house and going out into public. In the former case, abuse by a family member, you'll often have a phobia about remaining in the home.

P   And HOW might the identity of the abuser affect the treatment prescribed in Walter's case? (5)

W   If the abuser is a family member likely to remain in the household, you have to consider the drastic step of having the child removed from the home environment and at least temporarily placed in foster care. That's a big step, since it's so disruptive of the family unit; and you ordinarily wouldn't recommend that as part of the treatment except in cases of intrafamily abuse.

P   When you asked Walter about the identity of the abuser, WHAT did you tell him about your reason for wanting to know that? (6)

W   That's such a delicate subject that you want to try to put the patient at ease as much as possible. Before I put the question to Walter, I explained that my medical advice could depend on who had abused him. In very general terms, I told him that I'd make one type of recommendation if the person were a stranger and a different recommendation if the person were a friend or family member.

P   WHAT, if anything, did Walter say after you explained that? (6)

W   He said that he understood and that he'd tell me the truth about that just as he'd told me the truth about everything else.

P   Doctor Amar, WHO did Walter name as the person who had been abusing him?

W   His father, Paul Leslie.

P   To the best of your recollection, WHAT were Walter's exact words?

W   He began to sob, but he clearly said, "My daddy, Paul."

PART E.   Hearsay Exceptions Based on a Showing of Unavailability

§ 10.13 IN GENERAL

The preceding seven sections analyze hearsay exceptions recognized primarily because of an inference of the reliability of the hearsay statement. Other exceptions, though, depend to a greater degree for their recognition on a showing of necessity for resorting to the hearsay. These exceptions require proof of the declarant's unavailability at the time of trial. The following section discusses the test for unavailability in federal practice. § 10.14 through 10.16 then describe three hearsay exceptions requiring proof of unavailability as part of their foundation.

§ 10.14 THE UNAVAILABILITY OF THE DECLARANT AT TRIAL

[1] AT COMMON LAW AND BY STATUTE

At common law, the exceptions requiring proof of unavailability emerged at different times and developed varying tests for unavailability. Some exceptions demanded proof of the declarant's death, while others were satisfied by proof that the declarant was beyond the reach of compulsory process. The drafters of the Federal Rules elected a single, uniform definition of unavailability. Federal Rule of Evidence 804(a) sets out that definition:

> A declarant is considered to be unavailable as a witness if the declarant:
>
> (1) is exempted from testifying about the subject matter of the declarant's statement because the court rules that a privilege applies;
>
> (2) refuses to testify about the subject matter despite a court order to do so;
>
> (3) testifies to not remembering the subject matter;
>
> (4) cannot be present or testify at the trial or hearing because of death or a then-existing infirmity, physical illness, or mental illness; or
>
> (5) is absent from the trial or hearing and the statement's proponent has not been able, by process or other reasonable means, to procure:
>
> > (A) the declarant's attendance, in the case of a hearsay exception under Rule 804(b)(1) or (6); or
> >
> > (B) the declarant's attendance or testimony, in the case of a hearsay exception under Rule 804(b)(2), (3), or (4).
>
> But this subdivision (a) does not apply if the statement's proponent procured or wrongfully caused the declarant's unavailability as a witness in order to prevent the declarant from attending or testifying.

Under Rule 804(a), there are numerous methods of demonstrating the prior witness's unavailability. In the first three subsections of Rule 804(a), the witness is technically unavailable but actually present at trial (hearing #2). Under Rule 804(a)(1), the witness is deemed unavailable if the witness "is exempted from testifying about the subject matter of the declarant's statement because the court rules that a privilege applies." The prior witness from hearing #1 actually takes the stand in hearing #2, but the witness properly refuses to testify on the ground of privilege. Under Rule 804(a)(2), the witness is considered unavailable if he or she "refuses to testify about the subject matter despite a court order to do so." Here the witness does not have a legitimate ground for refusing to answer; but if the witness refuses to answer notwithstanding a court order to answer, as a practical matter the witness is unavailable. Under Rule 804(a)(3), the witness is unavailable if the witness "testifies to not remembering the subject matter."[5] Here too the witness is physically present, but as a practical matter the witness's testimony is

---

[5] Note that the judge need not find that the witness in fact cannot remember. According to the plain wording of the rule, it is sufficient the witness "testifies" to an inability to recall.

unavailable. When the proponent is relying on one of these three grounds to show unavailability, the proponent need ensure only that the witness's refusal or failure to recall is reflected on the record. The proponent should ask point blank about the topic of the prior testimony: "WHAT was the color of the defendant's car?" If the witness responds "I refuse to answer" or "I cannot remember," there is a sufficient showing of unavailability.

Rule 804(a)(4) declares that the prior witness is unavailable when the witness "cannot be present to testify at the trial or hearing because of death or a then-existing infirmity, physical illness, or mental illness." If the witness is now dead, the proponent may introduce a properly attested death certificate. The death certificate qualifies as an official record. If the witness is ill, under Rule 104(a), the jurisdiction may permit the proponent to prove the illness by a physician's affidavit, declaration, or letter. (Remember that in determining the existence of preliminary facts under Rule 104(a), the trial judge need not follow the technical exclusionary rules such as hearsay.) Otherwise the proponent may have to call the physician at hearing #2 to prove the illness of the prior witness. The proponent would have to lay the expert opinion testimony foundation outlined in § 9.03 of Chapter 9: the physician's qualifications, the physician's major premise, the basis of the expert's opinion, the ultimate opinion that the former witness is now too ill to appear and testify, and the expert's explanation of the opinion.

Finally, Rule 804(a)(5) announces that the former witness is considered unavailable if the witness "is absent from the trial or hearing and the statement's proponent has not been able, by process or other reasonable means, to procure" the witness's attendance or, under Rules 804(b)(2)-(4), the witness's attendance or testimony. In the case of the latter exceptions, the proponent must explore the possibility of deposing the declarant before the trial or hearing; even if the proponent cannot secure the witness's "attendance," a deposition hearing would enable to obtain the witness's "testimony" under oath." This subsection usually comes into play in two situations.

The first situation is the case in which the proponent simply cannot locate the former witness. The proponent could use a process server's testimony to establish the former witness's unavailability.

P   WHAT is your name?

W   Michael Senet.

P   WHERE do you live?

W   At 1440 Alsworth Street here in Alexandria.

P   HOW long have you lived there?

W   For the past five years.

P   WHAT is your occupation?

W   I am a process server.

P   WHERE do you work?

W   I work for the Speedy Process Service Company downtown.

P	HOW long have you worked there?
W	Three years.
P	HOW long have you been a process server?
W	Three years.
P	Mr. Senet, WHERE were you on the morning of January 17th of this year?
W	I stopped by your office.
P	WHY did you visit my office?
W	You had phoned and asked me to pick up a subpoena.
P	WHO was the subpoena for?
W	John Milton.
P	WHAT was his address?
W	Both the subpoena and the telephone directory listed his address as 40 Oxford Street, Apartment 201.
P	WHAT did you do after you picked up the subpoena?
W	I went directly to the address given.
P	WHAT happened when you arrived there?
W	I inquired whether he still lived there.
P	WHAT was the result of your inquiry?
O	Your Honor, I object to that question on the ground that it calls for hearsay.
P	Your Honor, may we approach the bench?
J	Yes.
P	Your Honor, I offer to prove that this witness will testify that the manager said Mr. Milton had moved. I want to use the testimony for a nonhearsay purpose under Rule 801(c)(2), its effect on the process server's state of mind. The issue is whether the process server acted reasonably and diligently. We have to judge his diligence in light of the information about Mr. Milton he was given by other persons such as the apartment manager.
J	The objection will be overruled.
P	Mr. Senet, let me repeat the question. WHAT was the result of your inquiry at Mr. Milton's apartment?
W	The manager said he had moved.
P	WHAT was Mr. Milton's new address?
W	Unfortunately, he did not leave a forwarding address.
P	WHAT did you do then?

W	Over the next few days I contacted other companies and agencies that might have Milton's new address.
P	WHICH companies and agencies did you contact?
W	To list just some, I talked to people at the telephone company, the gas company, the electricity company, and the welfare department.
P	WHAT was the result of your contact with these companies and agencies?
W	It was negative. None of them knew where I could locate Mr. Milton.
P	HOW many hours did you spend talking to people at these companies and agencies?
W	Over the period of days, I'd estimate I spent at least 10 full hours trying to hunt him down.
P	Mr. Senet, WHERE is Mr. Milton now?
W	I'm afraid that I have no idea.

The second situation is the case in which the former witness is in another jurisdiction. In some states, it is sufficient to show that the former witness is now beyond the reach of compulsory process. In the case of dying declarations and declarations against interest, the proponent must not only show that there was no compulsory process to compel the declarant's attendance at trial, the proponent must also show that he or she could not depose the deponent before trial. At hearing #2, the judge can, of course, judicially notice the constitutional and statutory provisions setting out the territorial limits of the court's compulsory process. In other states, the proponent must show not only that the former witness is now beyond the reach of compulsory process, the proponent must also show that the proponent unsuccessfully attempted to persuade the former witness to voluntarily attend hearing #2 or that any attempt would probably be futile. Federal Rule 804(a)(5) expressly requires the proponent to attempt to use "other reasonable means."[6]

Suppose that Mr. Watson has sued Ms. Belson for personal injuries resulting from a traffic accident. At the first trial of the case, Mr. Green testified on behalf of the plaintiff. Mr. Green was a passing acquaintance of the plaintiff and happened to be in the plaintiff's car at the time of the accident. The trial resulted in a judgment for plaintiff, but the defendant appealed. After the trial, Mr. Green moved from California to Minnesota. On appeal, the court reversed the judgment and remanded for a second trial. At trial #2, the plaintiff wants to use Mr. Green's former testimony. The plaintiff himself takes the stand to establish Mr. Green's unavailability.

P	WHO were your witnesses at the first trial in this case?
W	Myself, Officer Halston, and a Mr. Ted Green.

---

[6] Contrast the unavailability standard prescribed by Rule 1004(b) for the best evidence rule. Under that provision, it is sufficient that "an original cannot be obtained by any available judicial process." Unlike Rule 804(a)(5), 1004(b) does not require the proponent to resort to "other reasonable means."

P	WHERE does Mr. Green live now?
W	In St. Paul, Minnesota.
P	HOW do you know that?
W	For one thing, I've received letters from him postmarked St. Paul, Minnesota.
P	HOW do you know the letters came from Mr. Green?
W	I recognized his handwriting.
P	HOW did you recognize his handwriting?
W	I'm familiar with it. We worked together for several years, and I saw his handwriting on numerous occasions.
P	WHY else do you think he now lives in Minnesota?
W	I tried to contact him by telephone. I went through the operator in St. Paul and eventually reached him.
P	HOW do you know you were speaking with Mr. Green?
W	I recognized his voice just as I recognized his handwriting.
P	WHERE is Mr. Green today?
W	I don't know for sure.
P	WHERE was he when you last spoke with him?
W	In St. Paul.
P	WHY isn't he here?
W	He refused to come.
P	HOW do you know that?
W	I asked him to come during our last telephone conversation. He flat out refused and said he was too tied up with his business to come.
P	WHAT efforts have you made to persuade him to attend this trial?
W	I phoned him several times. I even volunteered to pick up the tab for his airline ticket. He just won't cooperate. He said that he doesn't want any more to do with trials and lawyers.

[2]   AS A MATTER OF CONSTITUTIONAL LAW

The Necessity for a Showing of the Unavailability of a Declarant of "Testimonial" Hearsay

The preceding paragraphs analyze the issue of unavailability from the perspective of the common law and modern statutes such as Federal Rule of Evidence 804(a). However, the Supreme Court has announced that in some cases, the Sixth Amendment confrontation guarantee imposes a separate requirement for a showing of the declarant's unavailability at trial.

Prior to 2004, the Court had generally restricted the scope of the constitutional unavailability requirement to hearsay exceptions that traditionally required such a showing at common law. The Court recognized that restriction in decisions such as *United States v. Inadi*, 475 U.S. 387, 106 S. Ct. 1121, 89 L. Ed. 2d 390 (1986) and *White v. Illinois*, 502 U.S. 346, 112 S. Ct. 736, 116 L. Ed. 2d 848 (1992).

However, the Court significantly altered the requirement in 2004 in its decision in *Crawford v. Washington*, 541 U.S. 36, 124 S. Ct. 1354, 158 L. Ed. 2d 177 (2004). There the majority declared that the confrontation clause imposes special restrictions on the prosecution's ability to introduce "testimonial statements." Writing for the majority, Justice Scalia stated that the Court was not providing a definitive, comprehensive definition of the expression. However, in his lead opinion the Justice gave several examples of statements that should be classified as "testimonial." To begin with, prior in-court testimony such as statements at prior trials, preliminary hearings, and grand jury hearings falls within the definition. Furthermore, the expression includes formalized out-of-court statements such as affidavits. Finally, Justice Scalia mentioned a third category. To give the reader a sense of the scope of this category, the Justice cited two formulations proposed in the briefs in *Crawford*. One was included in the amicus brief of the National Association of Criminal Defense Lawyers: "statements that were made under circumstances that would lead an objective witness reasonably to believe that the statement would be available for use in a later trial." The other was proposed by the Petitioner's Brief: "pretrial statements that declarants would reasonably expect to be used prosecutorially." The admissibility of a statement is no longer assured simply because the statement falls within a categorical hearsay exception recognized by common law or statute; the Sixth Amendment may bar the admission of the statement. The judge must make an ad hoc, case-specific determination whether the statement was testimonial in character.

Although some points of consensus among the commentators and courts have already emerged, there are still unsettled issues under *Crawford*. At one extreme, as Justice Scalia's opinion indicates, a statement by one coconspirator to another is not testimonial. If the police have lawfully intercepted and taped the statement, the confrontation clause does not bar its admission. At the other extreme, if a government attorney meets with an alleged victim at the prosecutor's office and, after "structured questioning," asks the victim to make a videotaped statement, the statement is testimonial. Likewise, the Supreme Court has ruled that formal certificates stating the results of forensic tests are testimonial. *Bullcoming v. New Mexico*, 564 U.S. 647, 131 S. Ct. 2705, 180 L. Ed. 2d 610 (2011) (a report certifying the results of a gas chromatograph test of a blood sample in a DWI case); *Melendez-Diaz v. Massachusetts*, 557 U.S. 305, 129 S. Ct. 2527, 174 L. Ed. 2d 314 (2009) (a certificate of a gas chromatography/mass spectrometry analysis of a suspected contraband drug). Decisions such as *Bullcoming* and *Melendez-Diaz* have brought some clarity to the law. However, the doctrine continues to evolve.

Statements made in the course of an "ongoing emergency." One of the battlegrounds in the cases has been statements by victims such as calls to 911 dispatchers and on-the-scene statements to police. In many cases, the prosecutor can make a prima facie showing that the statement would otherwise fall within Federal Rule of Evidence

803(1) or (2). However, if the declarant had calmed down and realized that he or she was speaking to a law enforcement agent, some courts characterize these statements as testimonial. In *Davis v. Washington*, 547 U.S. 813, 126 S. Ct. 2266, 165 L. Ed. 2d 224 (2006), the Court issued rulings in two related cases. One case involved a 911 call. The alleged victim made certain statements in a telephone conversation with the 911 dispatcher. Using primarily sentences with present tense verbs, the victim described what was then happening and called for help. The other case involved crime scene statements. Here the alleged victim made statements to an investigating police officer at the scene. After the police separated the victim from the suspected assailant, the victim used primarily sentences with past tense verbs to explain what the suspect had done to her. The Court held that the statements in the 911 call were nontestimonial but that the crime scene statements were testimonial. Justice Scalia elaborated:

> Statements are nontestimonial when made in the course of police interrogation under circumstances objectively indicating that the primary purpose of the interrogation is to enable police assistance to meet an ongoing emergency. They are testimonial when the circumstances objectively indicate that there is no such ongoing emergency, and that the primary purpose of the interrogation is to establish or prove past events potentially relevant to later criminal prosecution.

In *Michigan v. Bryant*, 562 U.S. 344, 131 S. Ct. 1143, 179 L. Ed. 2d 93 (2011), the Court expanded the concept of an ongoing emergency. In *Davis*, the Court had found an emergency still imperiling a domestic violence victim. In *Bryant*, the police discovered a shooting victim several blocks from the crime scene. The shooter was at large and perhaps still in possession of the firearm. Medical personnel attended to the victim during part of the police questioning. The Court found that the victim's statements to the police were nontestimonial. Writing for the majority, Justice Sotomayor stated that as in *Davis*, there was an ongoing emergency, in the instant case "extend[ing] beyond an initial victim to a potential threat to the responding police and the public at large." She insisted that it would be a mistake to "narrowly focus on whether the threat solely to the first victim had been neutralized because the threat to the first responders and public may continue." The police conversation with the victim included "the exact type of questions necessary" to assess the threat to their own safety and that of the public.

In *Ohio v. Clark*, 135 S. Ct. 2173, 192 L. Ed. 2d 306 (2015), the Court revisited the topic and further broadened the emergency concept. In *Clark*, a child made a statement to a teacher who was a mandatory child abuse reporter. The teacher noticed that the child had some injuries although the child was not complaining about them. The child answered the teacher's questions about the cause of the injuries. Although the state supreme court characterized the child's statements as testimonial, the Court reversed. Justice Alito delivered the opinion of the Court. While he stopped short of announcing that all statements to private parties are nontestimonial, the justice concluded that the child's answers to the teacher's questions were nontestimonial. In explaining his conclusion, Justice Alito pointed to several factors: The statements occurred "in the context of an ongoing emergency involving suspected child abuse," since at the end of the day the teacher had to decide whether to release the child back to a household that might include the child's abuser; during their "informal" conversation, the teacher did not suggest that the child's answers would be used to arrest or punish the abuser; and "[s]tatements by very young children will rarely, if ever, implicate the Confrontation Clause. Few preschool children understand the details of our criminal justice system."

Forensic reports. Despite *Bullcoming* and *Melendez-Diaz*, the admissibility of forensic reports remains problematic. The Court's subsequent decision in *Williams v. Illinois*, 567 U.S. 50, 132 S. Ct. 2221, 183 L. Ed. 2d 89 (2012) muddied the waters. In this rape case, the police sent a vaginal swab to Cellmark, a private laboratory conducting DNA testing. Cellmark extracted a male DNA profile from the sample and sent its report to the Illinois State Laboratory (ISP). At trial, relying on the Cellmark report, an ISP specialist testified. The question was whether the specialist's reference to the Cellmark report violated the Confrontation Clause. The prosecution argued that there was no violation because at trial, the report was used for the limited, nonhearsay purpose of showing the basis for the specialist's opinion. The fact situation sharply divided the Court.

—Four dissenters, led by Justice Kagan, argued that Cellmark's report was a testimonial statement that was clearly offered for its truth.

—Justice Thomas filed a concurrence. He agreed with the dissent that as a matter of logic, the report had been treated as substantive evidence admitted for its truth. However, he voted to affirm the conviction on the ground that Cellmark's report was too informal to qualify as a testimonial statement.

—Like Justice Thomas, a four-justice plurality, led by Justice Alito, voted to uphold the conviction. However, the plurality relied on a different rationale than Justice Thomas. The plurality reasoned that Cellmark's report was nontestimonial because the police had not identified a particular suspect at the time of Cellmark's test. That reasoning appeared to narrow the test and make it far more difficult to classify a statement as testimonial. Given the fragmented nature of the decision in *Williams*, the lower courts are understandably struggling with the application of *Crawford* to forensic reports.

The Sufficiency of the Showing of Unavailability

While *Crawford* changes the scope of the unavailability requirement, it does not purport to modify the standard for determining the sufficiency of a showing of unavailability. That standard is governed by *Barber v. Page*, 390 U.S. 719, 88 S. Ct. 1318, 20 L. Ed. 2d 255 (1968). Under *Barber*, the prosecution must establish that it made a good faith, diligent effort to bring the witness to the site of trial. A showing complying with Federal Rule of Evidence 804(a) will ordinarily satisfy *Barber* as well.

§ 10.15   DECLARATIONS AGAINST INTEREST

[1]   THE DOCTRINE

Statements or admissions of a party-opponent are disserving to the declarant's interest at the time of trial; the admission is inconsistent with some position the party-opponent is defending at the time of trial. So long as the statement is disserving at that time, it is admissible even if it was highly self-serving when made. Declarations against interest contrast with admissions in several respects. Declarations against interest are admissible only if at the time of the statement, the declarant believed the statement was contrary to his or her interest. The declarant's belief is the guarantee of the reliability of declarations against interest. Moreover, declarations against interest are admissible only if the declarant is unavailable at the time of trial. The declarant's unavailability supplies the necessity for resorting to the hearsay. In the case of admissions, the party-opponent is usually available and present at trial. Finally, the declarant of an admission must be the party-opponent while any person can make a declaration against interest.

Federal Rule of Evidence 804(b)(3) states the doctrine: "The following [is] not excluded by the rule against hearsay if the declarant is unavailable as a witness: A statement that: (A) a reasonable person in the declarant's position would have made only if the person believed it to be true because, when made, it was so contrary to the declarant's proprietary or pecuniary interest or had so great a tendency to invalidate the declarant's claim against someone else or to expose the declarant to civil or criminal liability; and (B) is supported by corroborating circumstances that clearly indicate its trustworthiness, if it is offered in a criminal case as one that tends to expose the declarant to criminal liability."

[2] ELEMENTS OF THE FOUNDATION

The foundation for this hearsay exception includes the following elements:

1. The declarant subjectively believed that the statement was contrary to his or her interest. Even at common law, the belief of the hypothetical, reasonable person could be used as circumstantial evidence of the subjective belief of the declarant. On its face, Federal Rule of Evidence 804(b)(3) refers only to the objective reasonableness test; and some federal courts have read the statute literally.[7]

   In applying this element, the courts focus on the specific statement proffered rather than the overall narrative including the statement. In *Williamson v. United States*, 512 U.S. 594, 114 S. Ct. 2431, 129 L. Ed. 2d 476 (1994), the Supreme Court announced that Rule 804(b)(3) permits the admission only of statements which are individually self-inculpatory; the rule does not authorize the introduction of collateral, non-self-inculpatory statements in the same narrative. For purposes of this exception, the unit of analysis is the individual hearsay assertion. The judge should separately test each assertion to determine whether it was disserving. For that reason, the proponent's question must be narrowly phrased to target the admissible statement. In *Lilly v. Virginia*, 527 U.S. 116, 119 S. Ct. 1887, 144 L. Ed. 2d 117 (1999), to a degree the Court essentially elevated the *Williamson* doctrine to constitutional status under the confrontation clause. Although *Lilly* does not mandate the use of *Williamson*'s assertion-by-assertion mode of analysis under the Sixth Amendment, *Lilly* does evince the same skepticism about the reliability of custodial statements

---

[7] *But see* United States v. Lozado, 776 F.3d 1119 (10th Cir. 2013) ("the actual knowledge of the declarant, when the evidence establishes it, is part of the 'reasonable person in the declarant's position' calculus. The reasonable person standard applies when proof of the declarant's state of mind is lacking").

that is also manifest in *Williamson*. If a person made a statement in police custody and the content of the statement suggests that the person was endeavoring to shift blame to the defendant, the Sixth Amendment may bar the introduction of the statement.

2. The interest was a recognized type of interest. All jurisdictions recognize pecuniary and proprietary interest, and most jurisdictions have expanded those categories to admit any statement that would subject the declarant to civil liability. Most jurisdictions now recognize penal interest, and roughly a fourth of the states admit statements contrary to social interest. However, the Federal Rules do not treat mere social interest as adequate.

3. The declarant is unavailable at the time of trial.

4. In some jurisdictions, if the defense offers a third party's confession to the crime the accused is charged with on the theory that the confession is a declaration against interest, there must be corroboration that the third party committed the crime. As Federal Rule of Evidence 804(b)(3) originally declared: "A statement tending to expose the declarant to criminal liability and offered to exculpate the accused is not admissible unless corroborating circumstances clearly indicate the trustworthiness of the statement." To eliminate a potential equal protection challenge to the statute, several courts read in the same corroboration requirement when the prosecution offers a declaration against interest against a defendant. The statute was later amended to prescribe the requirement for prosecution as well as defense evidence in Rule 804(b)(3)(B).

[3] SAMPLE FOUNDATION

Our fact situation is a robbery prosecution. The government alleges that the accused, Mr. Charles Bosley, robbed the Midland Stereo Store in New Orleans on February 17, 2017. The defense theory is that Mr. Gregory Bennett actually committed the robbery. During the defense case-in-chief, the defense called Bennett to the stand. Bennett refused to answer any questions about the robbery. His refusal would render him "unavailable" in most jurisdictions. As his next witness, the accused calls Mr. William Store. Mr. Store has already identified himself. The accused is the proponent.

P	WHAT is your occupation?
W	I am a member of the New Orleans Police Department.
P	HOW long have you held that position?
W	For about eight years.
P	WHERE were you on the morning of February 19, 2017?
W	I was on duty at the Dupont Street station.
P	WHAT happened while you were on duty that morning?
W	Some patrolmen brought in a suspect for questioning.
P	WHO was the suspect?

W	A Gregory Bennett.
P	WHEN was the last time you saw Mr. Bennett?
W	A few moments ago.
P	WHERE was he then?
W	He was on the witness stand. He's the witness who just left the stand.
P	WHAT happened after the patrolmen brought in Mr. Bennett?
W	As is my custom, I first informed him of his rights.
P	WHAT rights did you tell him about? (1), (2)
W	I told him he had a privilege against self-incrimination and a right to counsel.
P	WHAT was his condition when you informed him of his rights? (1)
W	He seemed O.K. He was alert, and there didn't seem to be anything physically wrong with him.
P	HOW did he react when you informed him of his rights? (1)
W	He seemed concerned.
P	WHAT did you do after you informed Mr. Bennett of his rights? (1)
W	I asked him if he understood his rights.
P	HOW did he respond? (1)
W	He said he understood them, and then he gave me some factual information I wanted.
P	WHAT did you do after you spoke with Mr. Bennett? (4)
W	I attempted to verify some of the facts Mr. Bennett had told me.
P	WHAT facts? (4)
W	He told me about the location of some of the stolen property, some receivers and speakers.
P	WHAT did Mr. Bennett say about the location of the stolen property? (4)
W	He said that several of the stolen receivers and speakers were in his apartment.
P	WHAT steps did you take to verify his statement? (4)
W	With his consent, I visited and searched his apartment.
P	WHAT did you find in his apartment? (4)
W	I found his personal effects. In addition, I found several receivers and speakers. I checked the serial numbers against the list supplied by Midland Stereo. The numbers matched.
P	Mr. Store, during your questioning of Mr. Bennett, WHO did he say robbed the Midland Stereo Store on February 17, 2017? (1)

112

O	Your Honor, I object to that question on the ground that it calls for hearsay.
P	Your Honor, may we approach the bench?
J	Yes.
P	Your Honor, I offer to prove that the witness will testify that Mr. Bennett confessed to the robbery my client is charged with. In light of the warnings Officer Store gave Bennett, Bennett must have realized his confession was contrary to his penal interest. There is corroboration that Bennett was involved in the robbery; some of the stolen property was found in his apartment. Finally, Bennett's refusal to answer makes him unavailable.
J	The objection will be overruled.
P	Officer Store, let me repeat the question. WHO did Mr. Bennett say robbed the Midland Stereo Store?
W	He said that he did.

§ 10.16   DYING DECLARATIONS

[1]   THE DOCTRINE

Another type of evidently sincere statement that is exceptionally admissible is a dying declaration. At early common law, the courts admitted the decedent's dying declarations in homicide prosecutions. The courts reasoned that there was a peculiar need for dying declarations in homicide prosecutions; the courts feared that if they excluded the victim's dying declaration, the murderer might go free. The circumstantial guarantee of the trustworthiness of dying declarations is the declarant's sense of impending death; at the point of death, the declarant should not have any reason to lie, and there is the theistic belief that the decedent will not want to face the Creator with a last lie on his or her lips. At common law, the necessity for admitting the hearsay is that at the time of trial, the declarant was dead.

The most arbitrary limitation on the common-law doctrine was its restriction to homicide prosecutions. Some jurisdictions now admit dying declarations in any type of criminal prosecution. Other jurisdictions admit such declarations in any type of case, civil or criminal. Congress decided to adopt a compromise view. Restyled Federal Rule of Evidence 804(b)(2) declares that "[t]he following [is] not excluded by the rule against hearsay if the declarant is unavailable as a witness: In a prosecution for homicide or in a civil case, a statement that the declarant, while believing the declarant's death to be imminent, made about its cause or circumstances." The most radical aspect of the Federal Rule is its abandonment of the requirement that the declarant be dead at the time of trial. The Federal Rule requires that at the time of trial, the declarant be "unavailable," as that term is defined in Rule 804(a). However, it is no longer necessary to prove the declarant's subsequent death.

[2]   ELEMENTS OF THE FOUNDATION

The common-law doctrine included the following foundational elements:

1. The case is a prosecution for homicide or a crime including homicide as an element. As we previously noted, many jurisdictions now admit dying declarations in other criminal prosecutions and civil actions. To determine whether this element is present, the trial judge looks to the indictment, information, or complaint; the charging pleading specifies the offense the defendant is on trial for.

2. The declarant is the victim named in the charging pleading. The witness must identify the declarant. The trial judge then examines the charging pleading to determine whether the declarant is the named victim. The consequence of this rule was that a declaration by decedent #2 was inadmissible in a prosecution for killing decedent #1 even if the defendant killed them at the same time and by the same blow. Many jurisdictions, including the federal courts, have abandoned this requirement.

3. At the time of the statement, the declarant had a sense of impending death. The declarant had abandoned all hope and concluded that certain death was imminent. The declarant sometimes voices his or her belief. The proponent may rely on such circumstances as the nature of wound, the administration of last rites, and statements made by third parties to the declarant.

4. At the time of trial, the declarant is dead. Under the Federal Rules, it is sufficient if the declarant is unavailable.

5. The statement relates to the event inducing the declarant's dying condition. The proponent usually asks "about" the cause of death. The statement may not describe previous quarrels or fights between the declarant and the defendant.

6. The statement is factual in nature. The early common law limited dying declarations to statements of observed fact. Modernly, the courts have relaxed the application of the opinion prohibition to dying declarations. The courts now admit conclusory statements such as the defendant killed the declarant "intentionally" or "without provocation."

At common law and under the Federal Rules, if the proponent can lay the above foundation, the dying declaration is admissible even though a criminal defendant did not have a prior opportunity to question the declarant. However, as previously stated, in *Crawford v. Washington*, 541 U.S. 36, 124 S. Ct. 1354, 158 L. Ed. 2d 177 (2004), the Supreme Court significantly altered confrontation clause analysis. There the majority announced that if a statement is "testimonial" in character, the prosecution must demonstrate both that the declarant is unavailable at trial and that the defendant had a prior opportunity to question the declarant. § 10.13[2] discusses the concept of "testimonial statements." It is true that in footnote 6, the *Crawford* majority acknowledged that in *Mattox v. United States*, 156 U.S. 237, 15 S. Ct. 337, 39 L. Ed. 409 (1895), the Court had upheld the admission of a dying declaration without imposing a requirement for a prior opportunity to question the declarant. However, at the end of the footnote, Justice Scalia added: "We need not decide in this case whether the Sixth Amendment incorporates an exception for testimonial dying declarations. If this exception must be accepted on historical grounds, it is sui generis." Some lower courts have already held that *Crawford* applies to dying declarations made under circumstances in which a reasonable declarant would have realized that the police would likely put the statement to prosecutorial use. However, the prevailing view is to the contrary.

[3] SAMPLE FOUNDATION

The fact situation is a homicide prosecution. The indictment alleges that the accused, Mr. James Ireland, murdered Ms. Grace Shafer. The indictment thus supplies the first element of the foundation. The prosecution calls Mr. William Turner as a witness. Mr. Turner has already identified himself. The prosecutor is the proponent.

P	Mr. Turner, WHAT is your occupation?
W	I am a physician.
P	WHERE are you licensed to practice medicine?
W	In three states, including here in New Hampshire.
P	WHERE were you on the morning of February 22, 2017?
W	I was in my office.
P	WHAT happened that morning?
W	I received an emergency call.
P	WHAT was the nature of the call?
W	Someone was hurt very badly, and they needed immediate medical attention.
P	WHAT did you do after you received this call?
W	I jumped in my car and drove to 1444 Garnet Street.
P	WHAT did you find there?
W	I found several police surrounding a very badly injured person.
P	WHO was that person? (2)
W	A Ms. Grace Shafer.
P	HOW do you know that? (2)
W	She identified herself, and I also checked the ID that she had in her purse.
P	WHAT condition was she in? (3)
W	Very bad. She had several stab wounds.
P	HOW many stab wounds? (3)
W	Five in her chest.
P	HOW deep were the wounds? (3)
W	Some were several inches deep.
P	HOW much blood was she losing? (3)
W	She was bleeding profusely.

P	WHERE was she bleeding? (3)
W	All over the chest area.
P	WHAT did you do after you discovered these wounds? (3)
W	I helped her as best I could; and when I realized that she was dying, I tried to make her as comfortable as possible.
P	WHAT, if anything, did you tell her about her condition? (3)
O	Your Honor, I object to that question on the ground that it calls for hearsay.
P	Your Honor, may we approach the bench?
J	Yes.
P	Your Honor, I offer to prove that the witness will testify he told Ms. Shafer that she was dying. I want to use that statement for a nonhearsay purpose as mental input under Rule 801(c)(2), namely, to show its effect on her state of mind. His statement helped produce a sense of imminent death in her mind. That is part of the foundation for the dying declaration I ultimately want to offer.
J	The objection will be overruled.
P	Doctor Turner, let me repeat the question. WHAT, if anything, did you tell Ms. Shafer about her condition? (3)
P	I was honest with her. She asked, and I told her she was dying.
P	HOW did she respond? (3)
W	She looked frightened. Then she sighed very deeply.
P	WHAT happened then? (3)
W	She asked that I contact a Catholic priest. She said that she wanted to receive the last rites of her church before she died.
P	WHAT happened then? (3)
W	The priest arrived and administered the sacrament. Then the priest and I accompanied her to the hospital.
P	Doctor, WHERE is Ms. Shafer now? (4)
W	She's dead.
P	HOW do you know that? (4)
W	She died in the ambulance on the way to the hospital.
P	WHAT, if anything, did she say about the cause of her death before she died? (5), (6)
W	She said someone had stabbed her with an ice pick.
P	WHO did she say stabbed her? (5), (6)
W	She said it was Jim Ireland.

§ 10.17 FORMER OR PRIOR TESTIMONY

[1] THE DOCTRINE

The next exception we shall consider is former testimony. As we noted in § 10.01 of this chapter, the primary rationale for the hearsay rule is that opponent has not had an opportunity to test the hearsay by cross-examination. What if the opponent had an opportunity to test the hearsay by cross-examination in a prior trial? Does that opportunity satisfy the hearsay rule and justify admitting the prior testimony in the present proceeding? Most courts have answered that question in the affirmative.

Federal Rule of Evidence 804(b)(1) states the doctrine:

> The following [is] not excluded by the rule against hearsay if the declarant is unavailable a witness: Testimony that:
>
> (A) was given as a witness at a trial, hearing, or lawful deposition, whether given during the current proceeding or in a different one; and
>
> (B) is now offered against a party who had—or, in a civil case, whose predecessor in interest had—an opportunity and similar motive to develop it by direct, cross-, or redirect examination.

The most controversial aspect of the doctrine has proven to be the requirement that the parties to the two hearings be identical. Early common law insisted upon complete identity of parties; the parties to hearing #2 were parties to hearing #1, and there were no additional parties at either hearing.

The common law quickly realized that the complete identity requirement was unnecessarily strict. So long as the present parties were parties to hearing #1, the courts concluded it was immaterial that there were additional parties to either hearing.

The courts then developed the modern "same party" view: The prior testimony is admissible *against* a party to hearing #2 if that party was a party to hearing #1. The courts focus on the party the testimony is now offered against, and they inquire whether that party had a fair opportunity to develop the facts at hearing #1 by direct or cross-examination. If the opponent had a fair opportunity to do so, it should not make any difference that the present proponent of the former testimony was not a party to hearing #1. The opponent had a prior opportunity to test the evidence, and that opportunity satisfies the purpose of the hearsay rule. Suppose that several passengers are injured when an airplane crashes during landing. In hearing #1, passenger A sues the airline and introduces the testimony of a safety engineer. During hearing #1, the airline can test and attack the engineer's testimony. Subsequently passenger B sues the airline. If the engineer dies prior to hearing #2, passenger B may use the record of the engineer's prior testimony against the airline. The "same party" view is the prevailing view in contemporary criminal cases.

In civil cases, most jurisdictions also recognize the "privity" view. Once again, the court begins its analysis by focusing on the party the testimony is now offered against. However, in the next step of analysis the court poses this question: Was the party the evidence is now offered against a party to hearing #1 *or* in technical privity with a party to hearing #1? The testimony is admissible against the party in hearing #2 if that party was a party to hearing #1 or in technical privity with a party to hearing #1, as in the case of successor owners of the same parcel of real estate. Since Federal Rule of Evidence 804(b)(1) uses the expression "predecessor in interest," some courts have construed the rule as codifying the "privity" view for civil cases. The statute uses the expression "motive" as well as "interest"; and these courts reason that if the drafters employed both terms, they must have intended that "interest" would mean something other than a mere similar motive.

Some courts and legislatures have taken a step beyond the "same party" and "privity" views; they recognize the "similar party" view. They still begin their analysis by focusing on the party to hearing #2 that the former testimony is offered against. However, they then pose a different question. Under the prevailing view, the pivotal question is whether that party had an opportunity in hearing #1 to probe the testimony. Under this new view, the question is whether there was *a* party to hearing #1 who had a similar motive to probe the testimony. The present opponent need not have had that opportunity; it is sufficient if there was a similarly situated party, a party with a motive and interest similar to that of the present opponent. To illustrate this view, we can revisit the last hypothetical. Suppose that in hearing #1, the airline had offered the testimony of a safety engineer against passenger *A*. The engineer dies before passenger *B* sues. Under this new view, at hearing #2 between passenger *B* and the same airline, the airline could use the engineer's testimony against passenger *B*. It is true that passenger *B* was not a party to hearing #1. However, passenger *A* was a party, and the two plaintiffs' motive and interest are sufficiently similar. We can assume with fair assurance that passenger *A* attacked the engineer's testimony as vigorously as passenger *B* would have. This view is the trend, but it is applied in only civil cases.

[2] ELEMENTS OF THE FOUNDATION

1. Hearing #1 was a fair, adversary hearing.
    a. The witness testified under oath.
    b. The opponent had an opportunity to cross-examine the witness.
    c. If the hearing was a critical stage in a criminal prosecution, the defendant was afforded the right to counsel.
2. There is substantial identity of issues between the two hearings. Although the courts often refer to issues in the plural, the best approach is to compare the issue the evidence was offered on in hearing #1 and the issue the evidence is now being offered on in hearing #2. The comparison of those issues largely determines whether there was a sufficiently similar motivation to develop the testimony in the two cases. In *United States v. Salerno*, 505 U.S. 317, 112 S. Ct. 2503, 120 L. Ed. 2d 255 (1992), the defense argued that the accused need not show substantial identity of issues when the accused invokes the exception against the prosecution and the prosecution could obtain the witness's live trial testimony by immunizing the witness. However, the Supreme Court rejected the argument. The Court noted that the text of Rule 804(b)(1) does not recognize any special exception for the criminal accused.
3. There is substantial identity of parties between the two hearings. Subsection 1,

supra, describes the split of authority on the test for substantial identity of parties.

    4.   At hearing #2, the witness is unavailable.

In many cases, the proponent will need two witnesses. One witness will establish the unavailability of the prior witness. The second witness will then describe the prior witness's testimony. The second witness may have been a spectator at hearing #1 who simply remembers the substance of the prior testimony; the witness need not be able to recite the testimony verbatim. It suffices if the witness can recall the substance of the witness's cross-examination as well as the direct testimony. Or the second witness may be the court reporter who describes the testimony with or without relying on notes. Finally, the proponent may entirely dispense with live testimony if the jurisdiction permits the authentication of the documentary record of hearing #1 by the court reporter's attesting certificate. In such a jurisdiction, the transcript is self-authenticating. The judge examines the transcript to determine whether the foundational elements are present.

[3] SAMPLE FOUNDATION

Assume that the proponent has already established the declarant's unavailability. In the following hypotheticals, the proponent is laying the other elements of the foundation.

We shall first illustrate the testimony of a spectator who happens to remember the substance of the witness's testimony at hearing #1. Our fact situation is a homicide prosecution. The government charges that Mr. John Gentile murdered his wife. An eyewitness to the killing, Mr. John Walton, testified at the preliminary hearing. Walton died after the hearing and before the trial. The prosecution has already proven Walton's unavailability by introducing a properly attested death certificate. Now the prosecutor calls Ms. Pamela Martin to lay the other elements of the foundation. The prosecutor is the proponent. Ms. Martin has already identified herself.

P	Ms. Martin, WHERE were you on the afternoon of March 12, 2016?
W	I was in another courtroom in this building.
P	WHAT were you doing there?
W	I was a spectator at a court proceeding.
P	WHY were you there?
W	I had read a lot about the case in the papers, and I was interested in watching it.
P	WHAT proceeding did you see the afternoon of March 12, 2016? (2), (3)
W	It was the preliminary hearing in this case.
P	WHO was there attending the hearing? (3)
W	For one, the accused himself, Mr. Gentile.
P	WHERE is Mr. Gentile now? (3)
W	He's in the courtroom right now.

P	Specifically, WHERE in the courtroom? (3)
W	Over there at the end of that table.
P	HOW is he dressed? (3)
W	He's wearing a blue suit, white shirt, and red tie.
P	Your Honor, please let the record reflect that the witness has identified the accused.
J	It will so reflect.
P	WHAT happened at this hearing you attended on March 12th? (1)
W	They called witnesses to testify.
P	WHAT did they do when they first called the witnesses to the stand? (1a)
W	They would swear them.
P	WHO questioned the witnesses? (1b)
W	Usually the prosecutor would start, and then the defense counsel would ask questions.
P	WHO asked questions on behalf of the defendant? (1c)
W	Some attorney. I honestly can't remember her name.
P	WHO were the witnesses that day?
W	There were three who stand out in my mind.
P	WHO were they?
W	A police officer named Strait, a doctor, and an eyewitness. The eyewitness was on the stand most of the day.
P	WHO was the eyewitness?
W	His name was John Walton.
P	HOW long was he on the stand?
W	About three hours.
P	HOW much of his testimony did you hear?
W	All of it.
P	HOW often did you leave the room while he was on the stand?
W	I didn't. I wanted to hear all of it. It was really exciting.
P	HOW well could you hear Mr. Walton while he testified?
W	Very well. I didn't have any problem hearing him.
P	HOW loudly was he speaking?
W	In a normal voice, but his voice carried well.
P	HOW close were you sitting to him while he was on the stand?
W	About 15 feet away. I was in the very first row for the spectators.

P	HOW well do you remember his testimony?
W	Very well. I was really enthralled. As I said, it was very exciting.
P	WHAT did he say during his testimony?
O	Your Honor, I object to that question on the ground that it calls for hearsay.
P	Your Honor, may we approach the bench?
J	Yes.
P	Your Honor, I concede that the testimony will be hearsay. However, it falls within the former testimony exception. The witness's testimony shows that there was oath, cross-examination, and counsel at the preliminary hearing. Since it was the preliminary hearing in this case, there's obviously identity of issues and parties. Finally, the death certificate shows that the former witness is now unavailable.
J	The objection will be overruled.
P	Ms. Martin, let me repeat the question. WHAT did Mr. Walton say during his testimony?

The proponent should now elicit all the important facts Walton previously testified to.

We shall now illustrate the use of a properly attested or certified transcript of the former testimony. To do so, we shall continue the same hypothetical. In this variation of the hypothetical, there is a documentary transcript of the preliminary hearing. We shall assume that the rule in this jurisdiction is that if the court reporter attaches a proper certificate to the transcript, the transcript is self-authenticating. Again, please assume that the prosecutor has already introduced Mr. Walton's death certificate.

P	Your Honor, I request that this be marked prosecution exhibit number seven for identification.
J	It will be so marked.
P	Please let the record reflect that I am showing the exhibit to the opposing counsel.
J	It will so reflect.
P	I now offer prosecution exhibit number seven for identification into evidence as prosecution exhibit number seven.
O	Your Honor, I object to the introduction of the exhibit on the ground that the exhibit is hearsay.
P	Your Honor, may we approach the bench?
J	Yes.
P	Your Honor, I concede that the exhibit is hearsay; but it is a properly certified transcript, and it falls within the former testimony exception.
P	Where is the foundation for the former testimony exception?

P   The transcript purports to be the record of the preliminary hearing in this case; there is obviously identity of issues and parties. I've already introduced Mr. Walton's death certificate, showing his unavailability. Page 2 of the transcript shows that the defendant had counsel at the hearing, page 16 shows that Mr. Walton was sworn before he testified, and page 142 shows that the defense had an opportunity to cross-examine Mr. Walton.

J   I agree. The objection will be overruled, and the exhibit will be received.

P   Your Honor, I request permission to read pages 22–53 to the jurors. I shall read the questions, and my clerk will take the witness stand and read the answers.

J   Permission granted.

§ 10.18   FORFEITURE BY WRONGDOING

[1]   THE DOCTRINE

After its enactment, Rule 804 was amended to include a new subdivision (b)(6), now reading: "The following [is] not excluded by the rule against hearsay if the declarant is unavailable as a witness: A statement offered against a party that wrongfully caused—or acquiesced in wrongfully causing—the declarant's unavailability as a witness, and did so intending that result."

In the 1980s and early 1990s, the federal courts began developing a line of authority recognizing the proposition that an accused waives his or her rights under the confrontation clause by killing an adverse witness or otherwise rendering the witness unavailable to testify at trial. The drafters of the amendment reasoned that if such wrongdoing could forfeit constitutional rights, *a fortiori* it should result in a forfeiture of a litigant's rights under the statutory hearsay rule. Moreover, although the federal decisions in question were criminal cases, the amendment applies in civil cases as well as prosecutions.

[2]   ELEMENTS OF THE FOUNDATION

1.   A certain person was a potential witness in a particular proceeding. If a witness list had been filed in the case, the court could judicially notice the witness list.

2.   Someone contacted the potential witness.

3.   The purpose of the contact was to procure the person's unavailability as a witness in the proceeding. If the third party announced his or her intent, the statement would be exceptionally admissible as an assertion of state of mind under Rule 803(3). Moreover, if the third party is the party-opponent in the litigation, any relevant statement would be admissible nonhearsay under Rule 801(d)(2)(A). Initially, some commentators distinguished the confrontation clause standard from the test under Rule 804(b)(6). Richard D. Friedman, *Adjusting to* Crawford: *High Court Decision Restores Confrontation Clause Protection*, 19 CRIM. JUST. 4, 12 (Summer 2004). On the one hand, it is arguable that the defendant should be held to have forfeited his or her Sixth

Amendment rights whenever he or she causes the witness's unavailability. Thus, if the defendant killed a victim in the heat of passion, the confrontation clause would not bar the admission of the victim's statements even though in the fit of anger the defendant gave no thought at all to rendering the victim unavailable as a witness. On the other hand, the wording of the statute, "intended to," appears to prescribe an intent requirement. In *Giles v. California*, 554 U.S. 353, 128 S. Ct. 2678, 171 L. Ed. 2d 488 (2008), the Supreme Court held that a defendant forfeits his or her confrontation clause rights only if the defendant's conduct is designed to prevent the potential witness from testifying.

4. The contact rendered the potential witness unavailable. Unavailability would be clear if the third party killed the person. However, unavailability can take other forms. For example, if, immediately after a threat, the potential witness stated that he or she intended to leave the jurisdiction and avoid appearing at trial, under Rule 803(3) the statement would be admissible both to prove the witness's then existing intent and the fact that they later carried out that intention. Moreover, the natural tendency of a threat would be to cause the potential witness to absent himself or herself from trial; and if the witness made the statement immediately after the threat, there would be a common-sense inference that the threat caused the potential witness to become unavailable.

5. The third party's conduct was imputable to the party the declarant's statement is offered against. The conduct would be imputable if:

    a. The third party was the party to the proceeding; or

    b. The party authorized the third party to contact the potential witness and cause the witness's unavailability; or

    c. After the third party's contact with the potential witness, the party learned of the third party's conduct and acquiesced in it.

[3] SAMPLE FOUNDATION

Assume that the proponent has already established that Grant Couch was a potential witness in a trial and that Couch was unavailable at the time of trial. In the following hypothetical, the proponent is laying the other elements of the foundation. The witness has already made an in-court identification of the defendant.

P   WHERE were you on the afternoon of April 13, 2017?

W   I was at the defendant's house.

P   WHO else was there? (2), (5)

W   Grant Couch.

P   HOW do you know that the other person was Grant Couch?

W   I've known him for years. We went to high school together. Grant, the defendant, and I have known each other since high school.

P   WHAT, if anything, did the defendant say to Mr. Couch? (3)

W	He threatened him.
P	Please be more specific. To the best of your recollection, WHAT did the defendant say? (3)
W	He told Grant that he'd heard that Grant was going to testify against him in his pending drug case. He added that if Grant took the stand, he, the defendant, would "blow him away."
P	HOW did Grant react when the defendant said that? (4)
W	He turned pale as a ghost and started shaking.
P	WHAT, if anything, did Grant say to the defendant? (4)
W	He told the defendant that he, Grant, would "get out of town right away" and that the defendant would "never have to lay eyes on" him again.
P	WHAT did Grant do then? (4)
W	He immediately stood up and virtually ran out the door. He jumped in his car and sped away.

PART F.   The Residual Hearsay Exception Based on Showings of Reliability and Necessity

§ 10.19   THE RESIDUAL HEARSAY EXCEPTION

[1]   THE DOCTRINE

The list of hearsay exemptions and exceptions in §§ 10.03–10.17 of this chapter is incomplete. In the first place, the Federal Rules enumerate other hearsay exceptions. For example, Rules 803(13) and 804(b)(4) create exceptions for certain statements about family history. Rules 803(14)–(15) set out exceptions relating to documents affecting property interests. Rule 803(16) recognizes an exception for ancient documents, 803(17) another exception for market reports, and 803(22) still another exception for judgments.

However, the list is incomplete in a second, more fundamental sense. The Rules explicitly confer residual discretion on the trial judge to admit hearsay that falls outside the enumerated exceptions. Prior to December 1, 1997, the discretion was set out in Rules 803(24) and 804(b)(5). Effective December 1, 1997, the two statutes were merged into Rule 807. That Rule now reads:

> (a)   In General. Under the following circumstances, a hearsay statement is not excluded by the rule against hearsay even if the statement is not specifically covered by a hearsay exception in Rule 803 or 804:
>
> > (1)   the statement has equivalent circumstantial guarantees of trustworthiness;
> >
> > (2)   it is offered as evidence of a material fact;
> >
> > (3)   it is more probative on the point for which it is offered than any other

evidence that the proponent can obtain through reasonable efforts; and

    (4)   admitting it will serve the purposes of these rules and the interests of justice.

  (b)   Notice. The statement is admissible only if, before the trial or hearing, the proponent gives an adverse party reasonable notice of the intent to offer the statement and its particulars, including the declarant's name and address, so that the party has a fair opportunity to meet it.

In 2019, Rule 807 was amended again. The Rule now reads:

    (a) General Rule. Under the following circumstances, a hearsay statement is not excluded by the rule against hearsay even if the statement is not specifically covered by a hearsay exception in Rule 803 or 804:

    (1)   the statement is supported by sufficient guarantees of trustworthiness—after considering the totality of circumstances under which it was made and evidence, if any, corroborating the statement; and

    (2) it is more probative on the point for which it is offered than any other evidence that the proponent can obtain through reasonable efforts.

    (b) Notice. The statement is admissible only if the proponent gives an adverse party reasonable notice of the intent to offer the statement—including its substance and the declarant's name—so that the party has a fair opportunity to meet it. The notice must be provided in writing before the trial or hearing—or in any form during the trial or hearing if the court, for good cause, excuses a lack of earlier notice.

The amendment effects several changes to Rule 807. To begin with, the amendment eliminates the prior reference to "equivalent circumstantial guarantees." Under the prior language, several courts had adopted a "near miss" doctrine, namely, that a statement proffered under Rule 807 was automatically inadmissible if the statement came close to but fell just short of satisfying the requirements of a Rule 803 or 804 exception. However, the May 24, 2018 report of the Evidence Advisory Committee interprets the "sufficient guarantees" language in the amendment as meaning that "a statement that nearly misses a standard exception can be admissible under Rule 807 so long as the court finds that there are sufficient guarantees of trustworthiness." Moreover, the amendment resolves the previous split of authority over the question of whether the judge could consider corroborating evidence in deciding whether the statement was reliable enough to be admissible. In addition, the pretrial notice must now be "in writing." However, the Committee on Rules of Practice and Procedure report on the amendment states that the writing requirement "is satisfied by notice in electronic form." Finally, the amendment eliminates the need for the notice to state the declarant's address.

During the mid-1970s and early 1980s, most courts applied the residual exceptions conservatively. However, in the mid-1980s, some courts became more receptive to invocations of the residual exceptions. One of the battlegrounds was the admissibility of transcripts of the grand jury testimony of deceased witnesses. Since even the target of the grand jury investigation does not have a right to cross-examine at the hearing, the grand jury testimony cannot be admitted as former testimony under Rule 804(b)(1). If the testimony is going to be admitted, it must be introduced, if at all, under the residual exception. Prior to 2004, there were numerous decisions admitting grand jury testimony on that theory under Rule 807's predecessor, 804(b)(5). However, grand jury testimony is undeniably a "testimonial statement" as the majority used that expression in *Crawford v. Washington*, 541 U.S. 36, 124 S. Ct. 1354, 158 L. Ed. 2d 177 (2004). Indeed, Justice Scalia expressly used grand jury testimony as one of his examples. Thus, *Crawford* curtailed the judicial trend to admit grand jury testimony under the residual exception in criminal cases.

[2] ELEMENTS OF THE FOUNDATION

Under the residual exception, the proponent must lay the following foundation:

1. The proponent gave the opposition adequate, advance notice of the tenor of the hearsay statement and the proponent's intention to offer the statement at trial.

2. The statement was reliable. Again, by virtue of the 2019 amendment, the proponent need not show that the statement possesses circumstantial guarantees of trustworthiness "equivalent" to those of a Rule 803 or 804 exception. The standard is now whether the statement has "sufficient guarantees of trustworthiness." It is ideal if the proponent shows that there was little possibility of insincerity or of flaws in the declarant's perception, memory, or narrative ability. The courts tend to place the greatest stress on the factor of the declarant's sincerity; if there is a common-sense reason to believe that the declarant was speaking sincerely, that factor cuts strongly in favor of admitting the statement. The proponent can show that there was a factor present giving the declarant a positive motivation for sincerity, as in the case of the nervous excitement making startled declarations admissible. Alternatively, the proponent can show that there was a factor present creating a disincentive for lying, as in the case of the disserving quality of declarations against interest.

3. There is some necessity for resorting to the hearsay. At the very least there should be the relative necessity required by Rule 803: the out-of-court statement is more likely to be reliable than any testimony now available from the same source. The case is stronger when the necessity is absolute, that is, unavailability satisfying Rule 804(a).

[3] SAMPLE FOUNDATION

The hypothetical fact situation is a civil wrongful death action. The plaintiff alleges that the accused Nelson was speeding, ran a red light, and struck a pedestrian named Garner, the plaintiff's husband. Garner died as a result of the injuries he sustained. A month after the accident, the grand jury conducted an investigation into the accident and indicted Nelson. An eyewitness, Mr. West, testified at the hearing. At the hearing, West identified the defendant's car and testified positively that the defendant ran the red light. West died unexpectedly after the hearing and before trial. The plaintiff has made a motion *in limine* in the nature of a motion to admit the transcript of West's grand jury testimony. Under the rules of court in this jurisdiction, at these hearings the judge receives affidavits rather than hearing live testimony. The following is the oral argument on the motion:

J   I'm prepared to hear argument on the motion. Ms. Plaintiff, are you ready to proceed?

P   Certainly, Your Honor. Your Honor, let me say at the outset that we realize that we cannot offer Mr. West's testimony under Rule 804(b)(1); the defendant didn't have an opportunity to cross at the grand jury hearing, and we therefore can't offer the transcript as former testimony.

However, we believe very strongly that this is an appropriate case for admitting the testimony under the residual exception, Rule 807. To begin with, we've complied with the advance notice requirement. (1) We served notice of this motion on the defense more than two weeks ago. There is a copy of the service in the court file. To make sure that the defense understood exactly what we intended to offer, we attached a Xerox copy of the relevant pages of the transcript to the notice of motion.

J   Mr. Defense Attorney, would you like to be heard?

O   I certainly would, Your Honor. I'll be brief.

First, we don't believe that this is a proper use of Rule 807. On pages two and three of our memorandum of law, we've noted the many cases stating that Congress intended the residual exceptions to be used sparingly. Even more to the point, page four of the memo lists the cases specifically holding that the exception does not apply to grand jury transcripts. We urge you to follow those cases.

J   Ms. Plaintiff, do you have any response?

P   Yes, Your Honor. I'll also try to be brief.

We acknowledge that there are cases urging a narrow interpretation of the residual exception and even cases specifically rejecting grand jury transcripts offered under the exceptions. However, we'd ask you to note that all the cases cited in the defense memorandum were decided in the late 1970s. On page three of our memorandum, we conceded that until the early 1980s, the trend in the case law was toward a narrow interpretation of the residual exception. However, pages four through seven of our memorandum cite more recent decisions. After carefully considering the legislative history of the residual exception, those decisions adopt a more expansive interpretation of the residual exception, and many cases now admit grand jury transcripts. This is a civil case, and consequently confrontation clause concerns are inapplicable.

J   I agree. The motion to admit will be granted.

Bibliography

"Trial Evidence Skills Manual." by Hallahan, Tim. pp. 1-28. Published Summer 2023, (author) Hallahan, Tim, 2023. (28 pages).

"Chapter 10: The Hearsay Rule, Its Exemptions, and Its Exceptions." In Evidentiary Foundations, 11e, by Imwinkelried, Edward. pp. 447-545. Carolina Academic Press, 2020. (99 pages).

These course materials were produced by XanEdu
and are intended for your individual use. If you have
any questions regarding these materials, please contact:

XanEdu Customer Support
support@xanedu.com
1-888-212-3121

XanEdu works to inspire the education community
with innovative solutions to build affordable, accessible
learning experiences that drive student success.

XanEdu, Inc.

www.xanedu.com

CPID: 1502723
ISBN 979-8-8227-2660-4

9 798822 726604